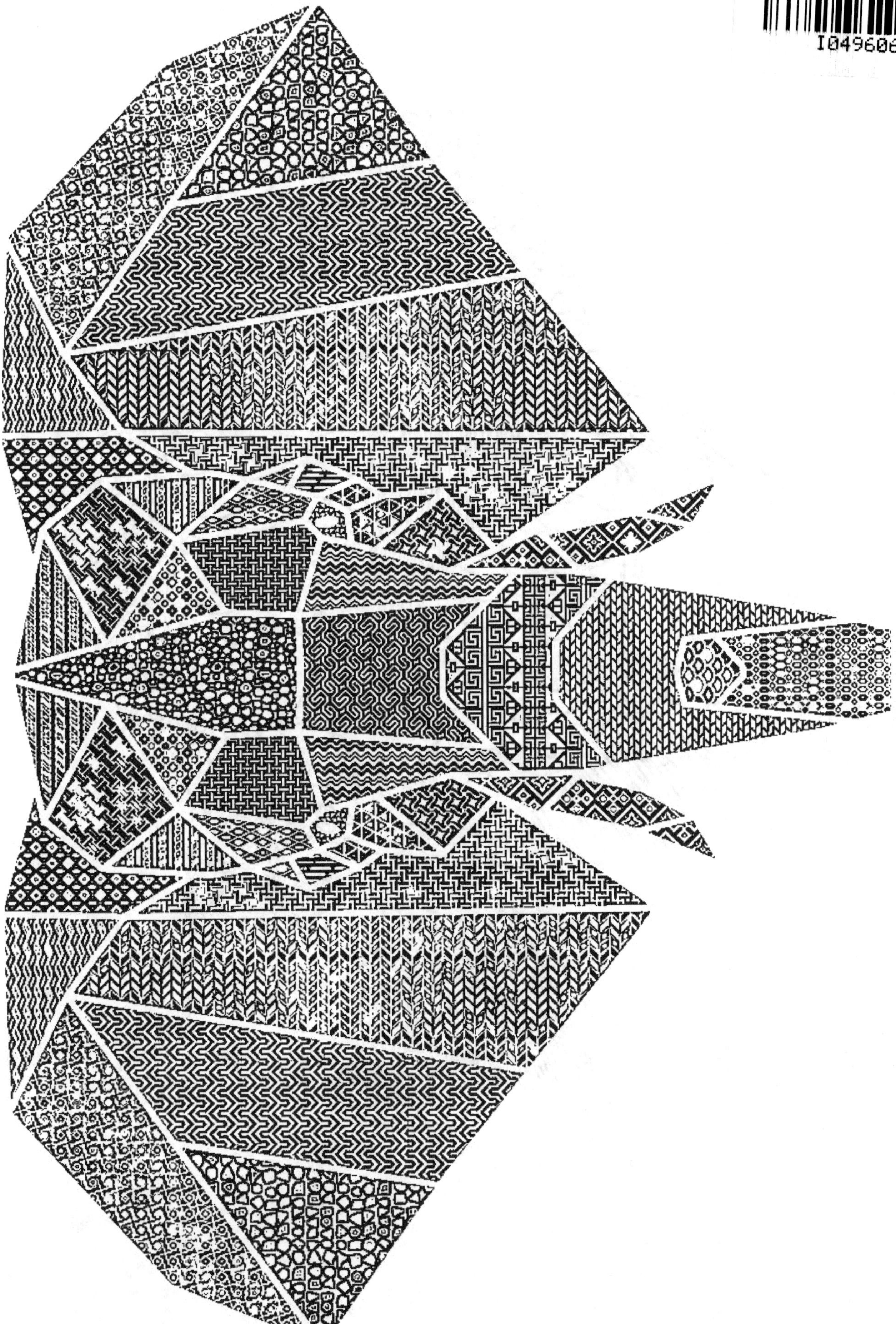

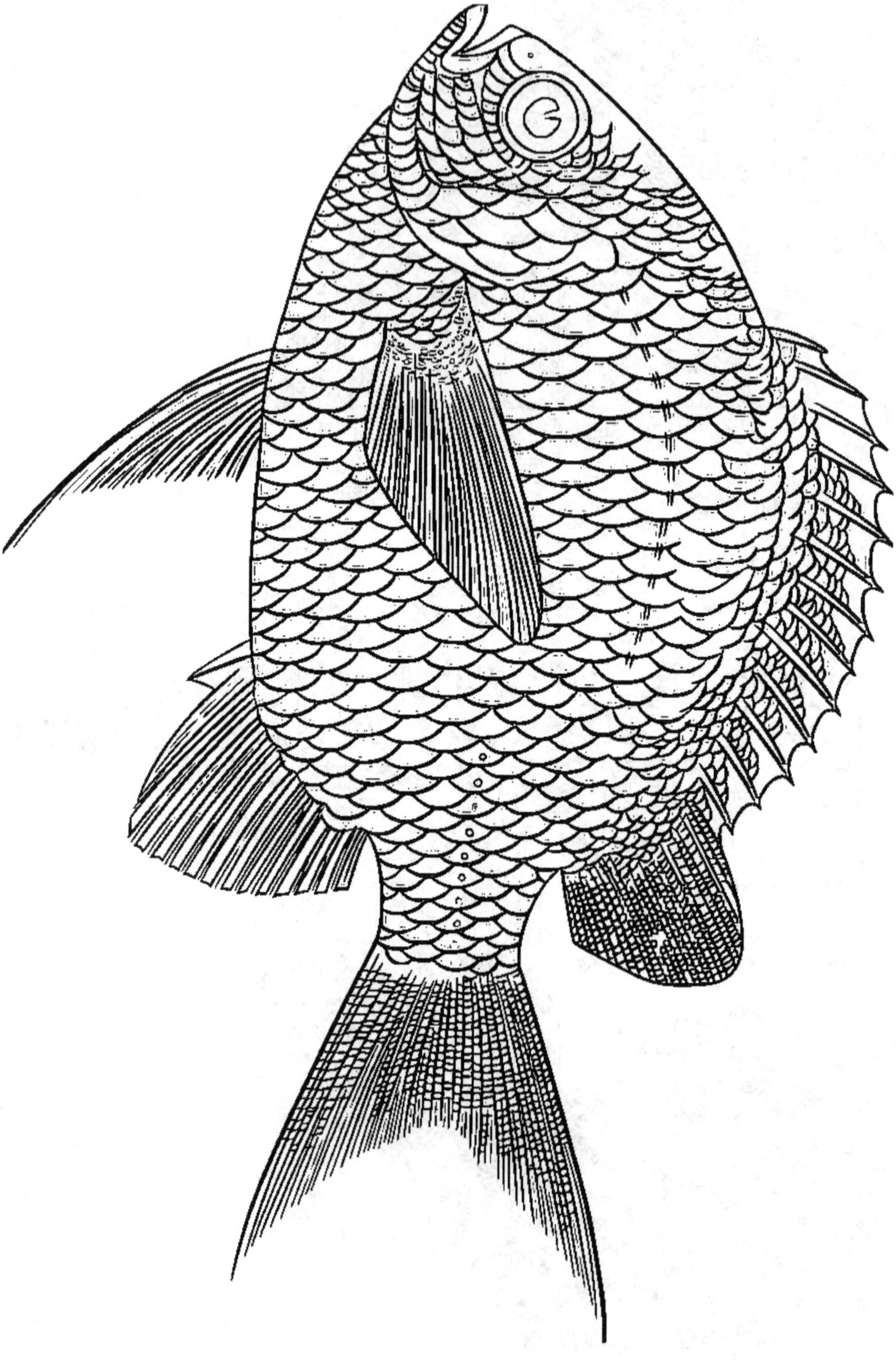

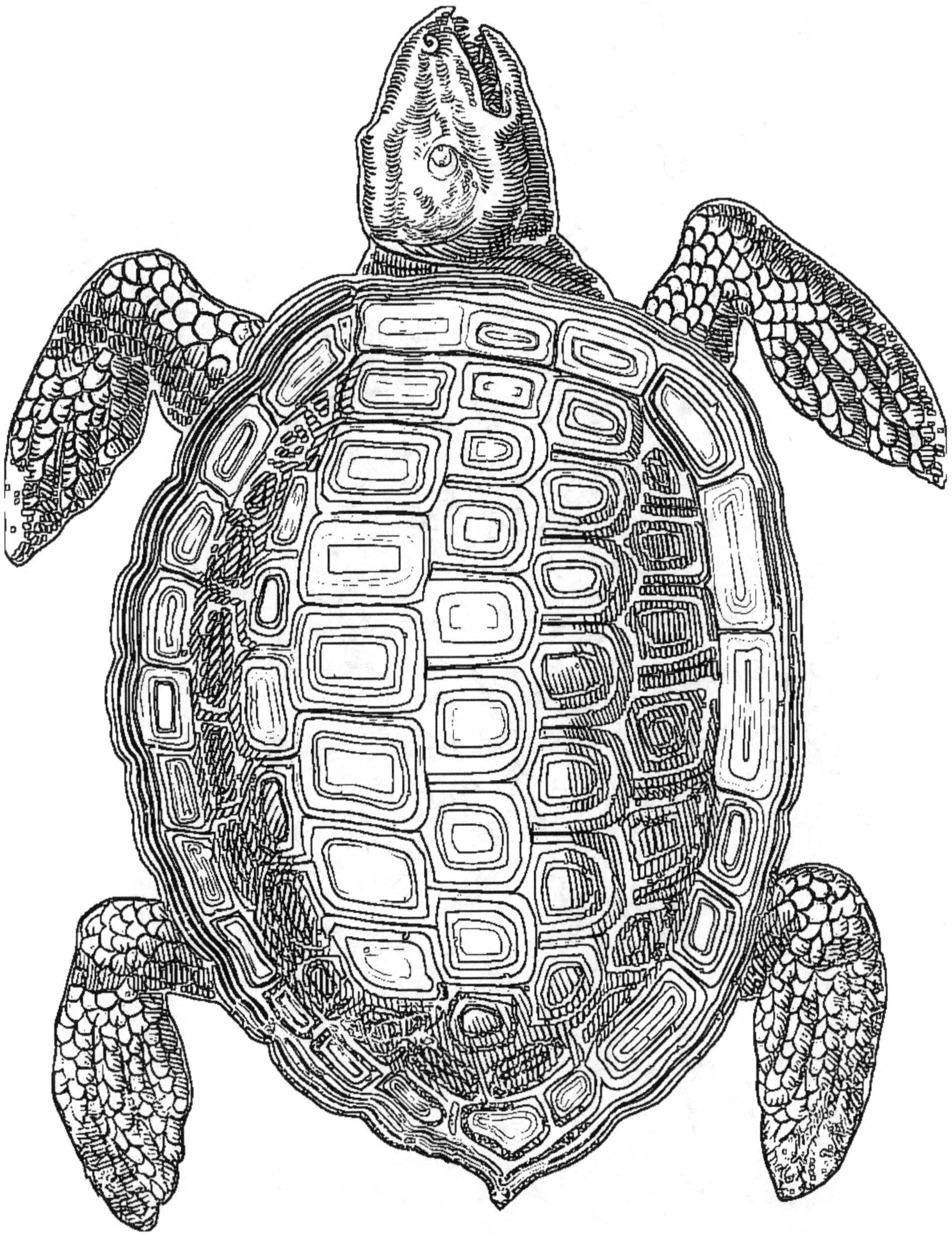

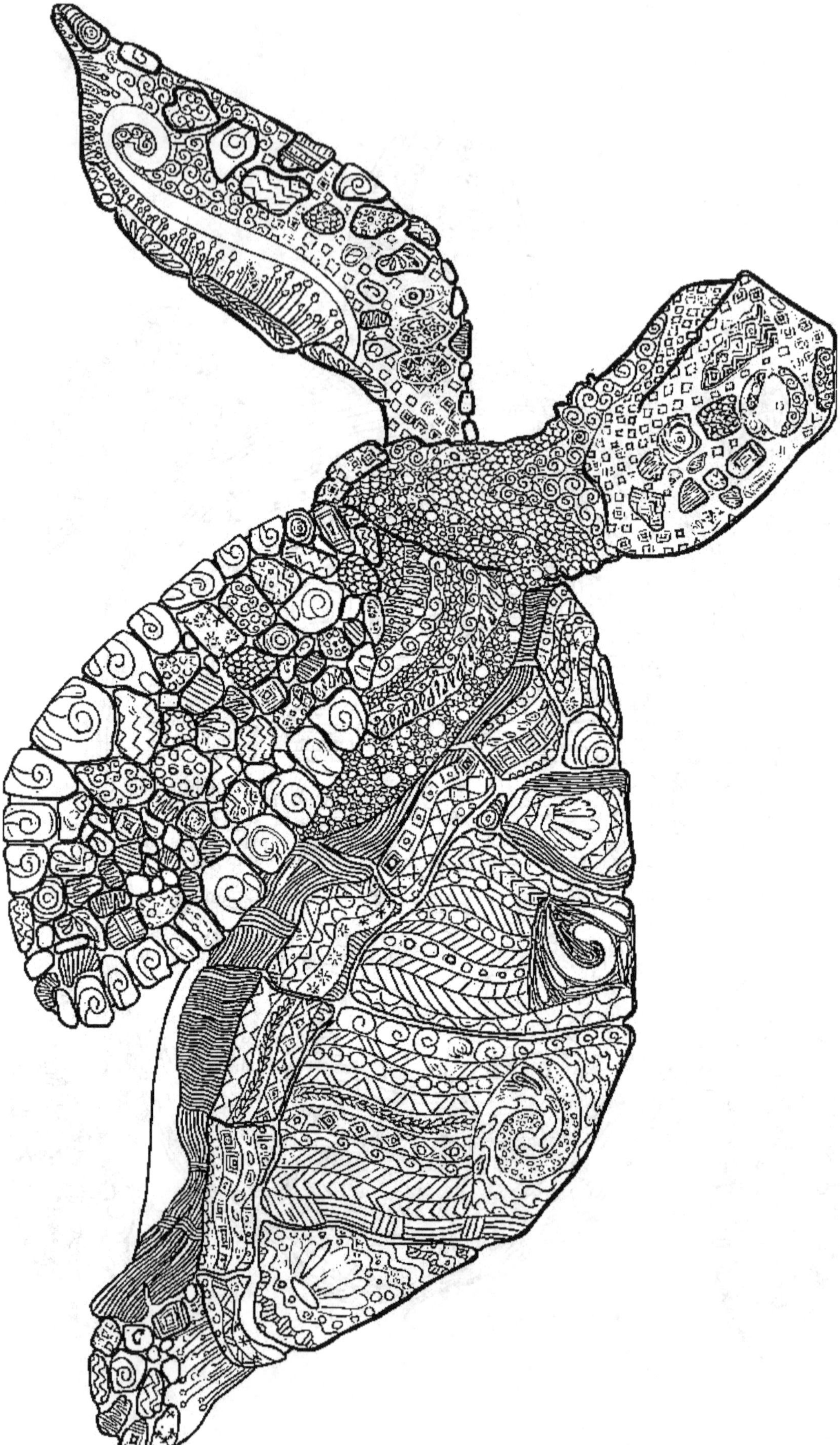

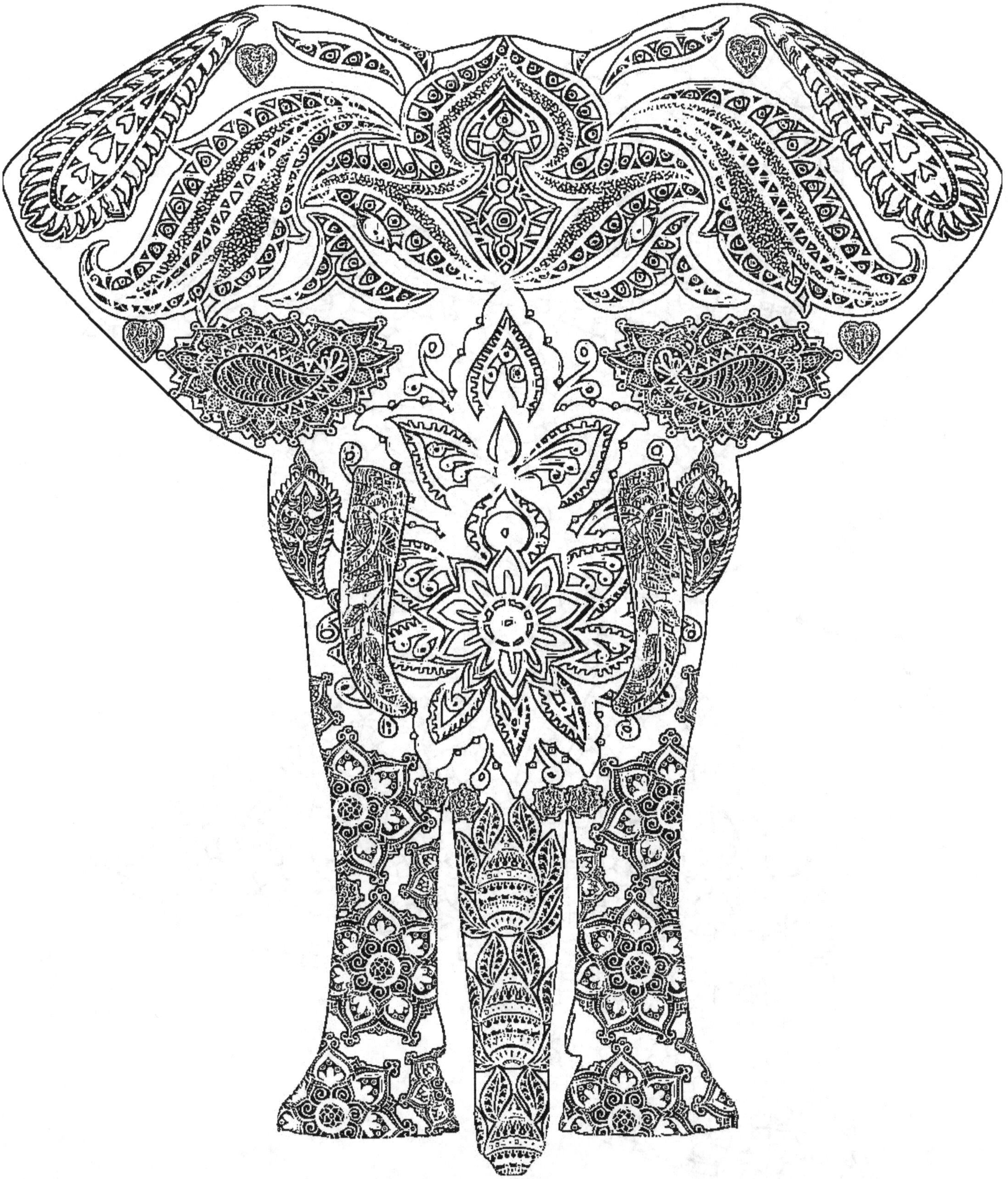

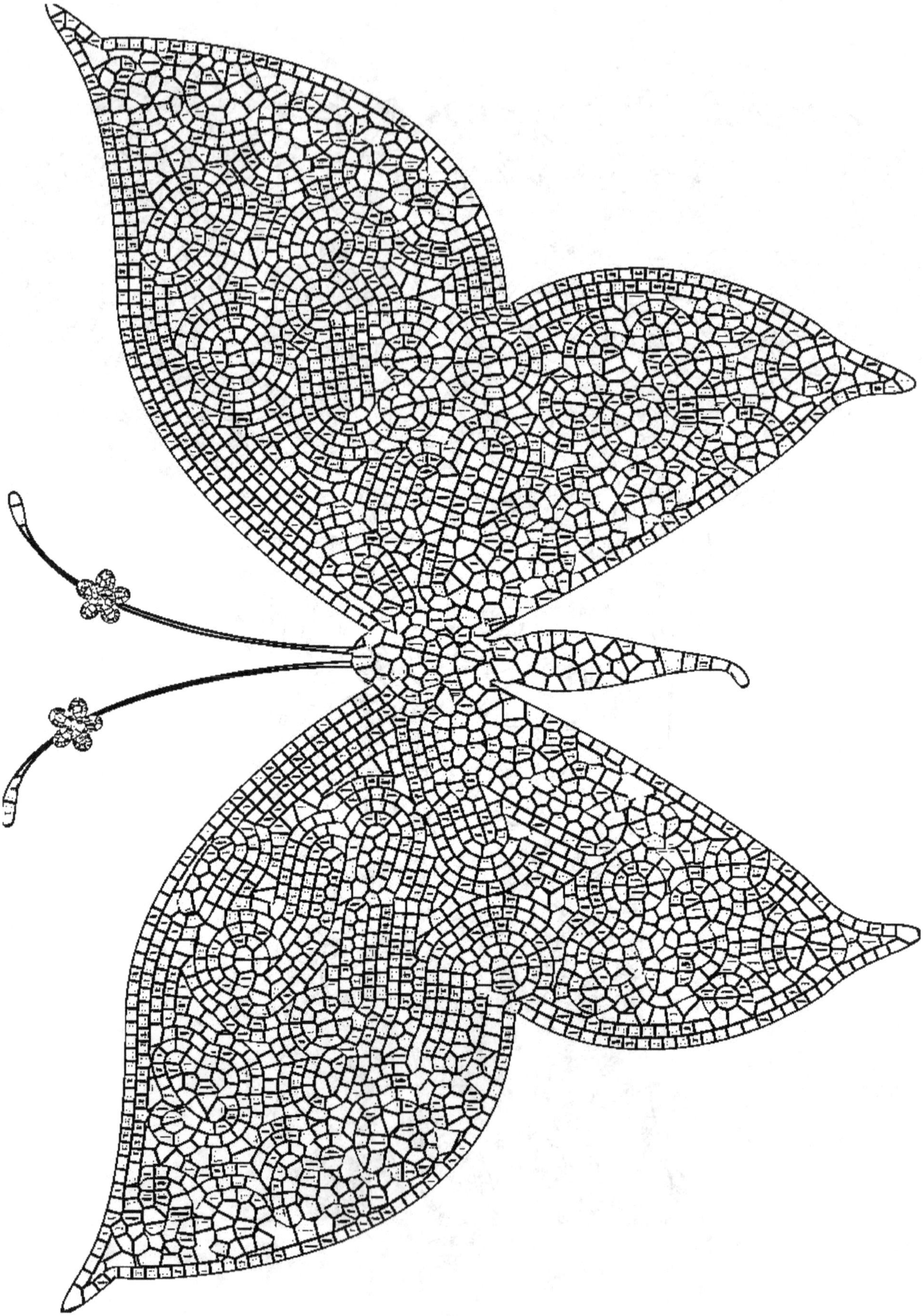

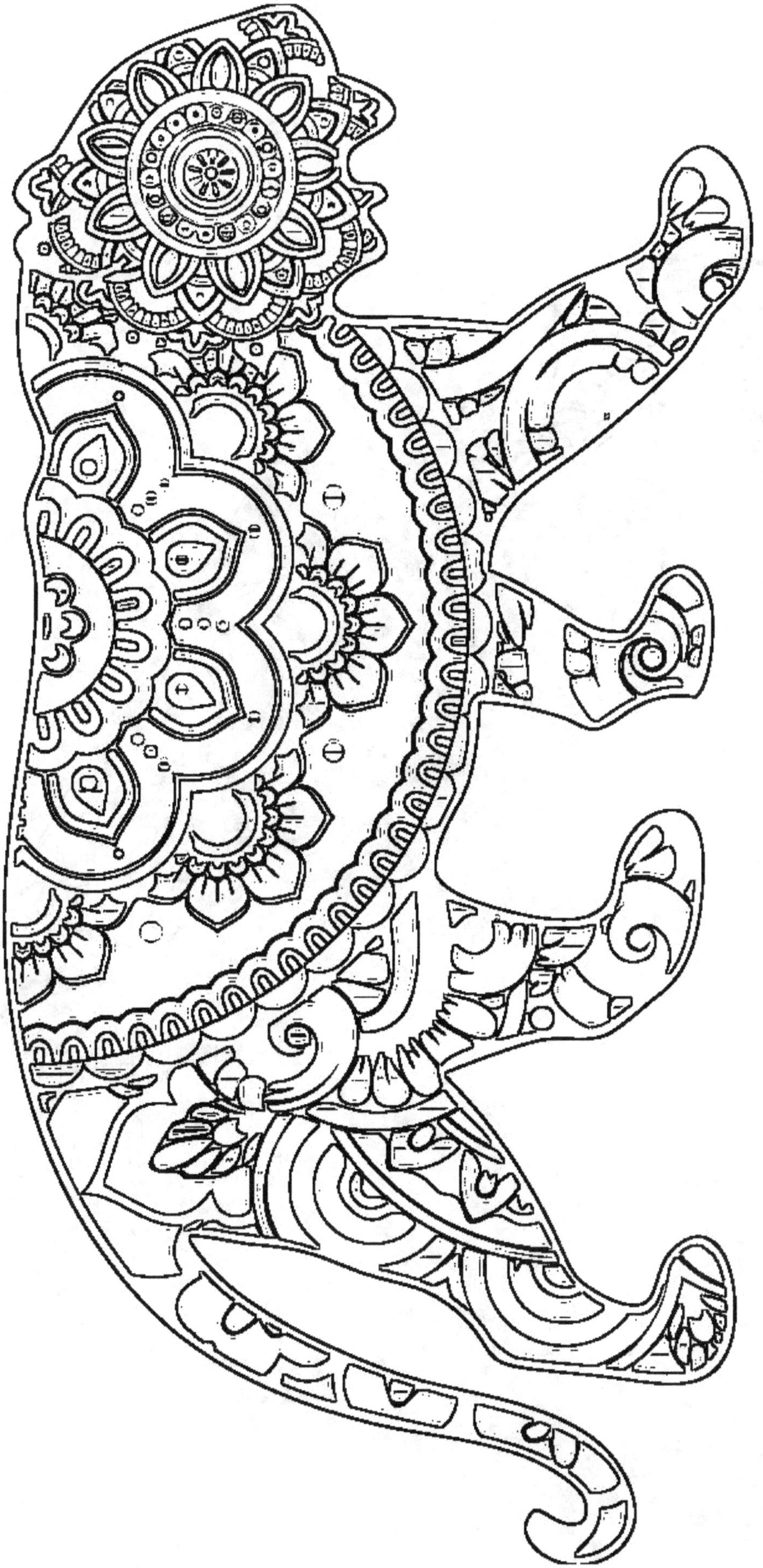

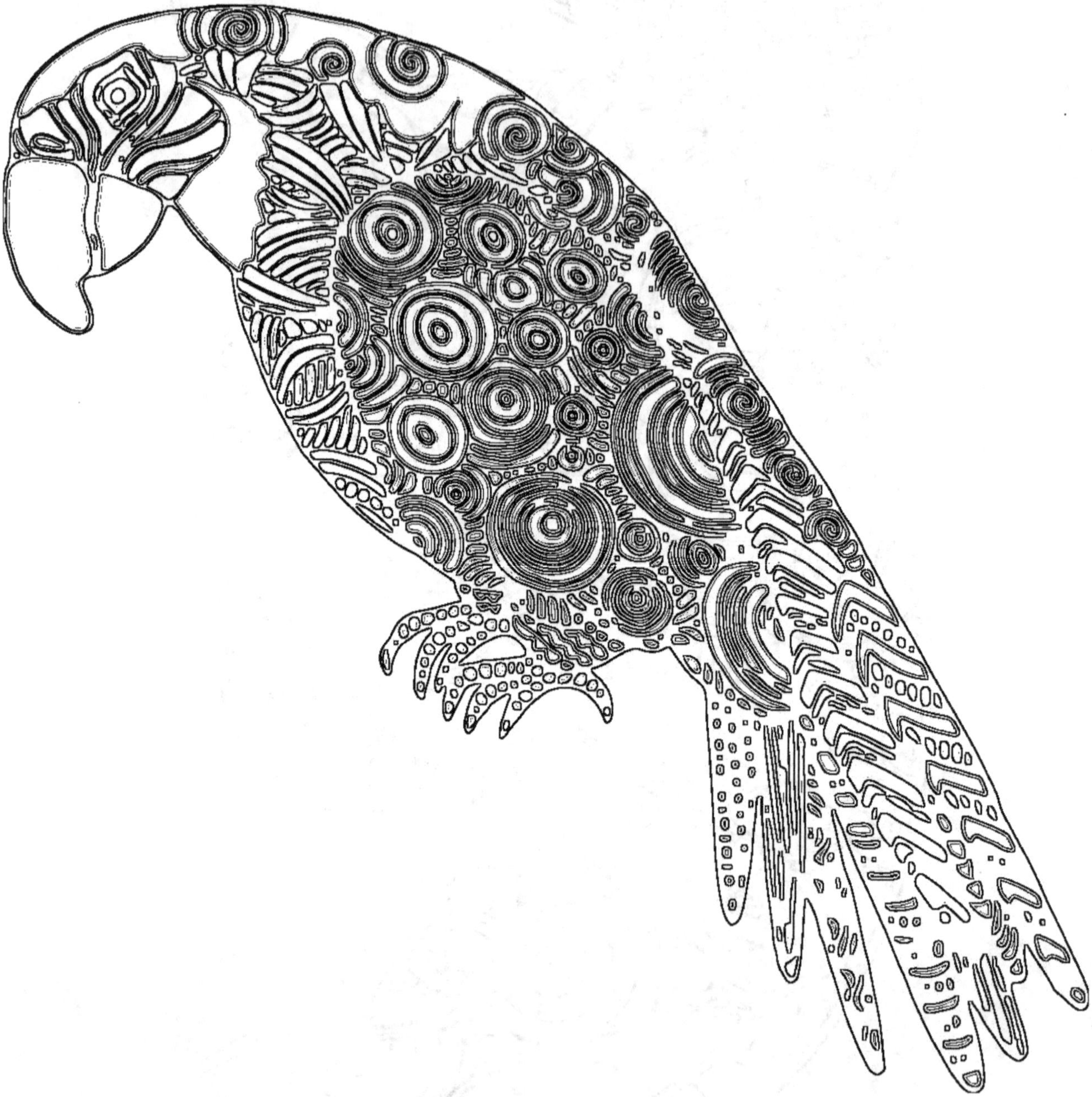

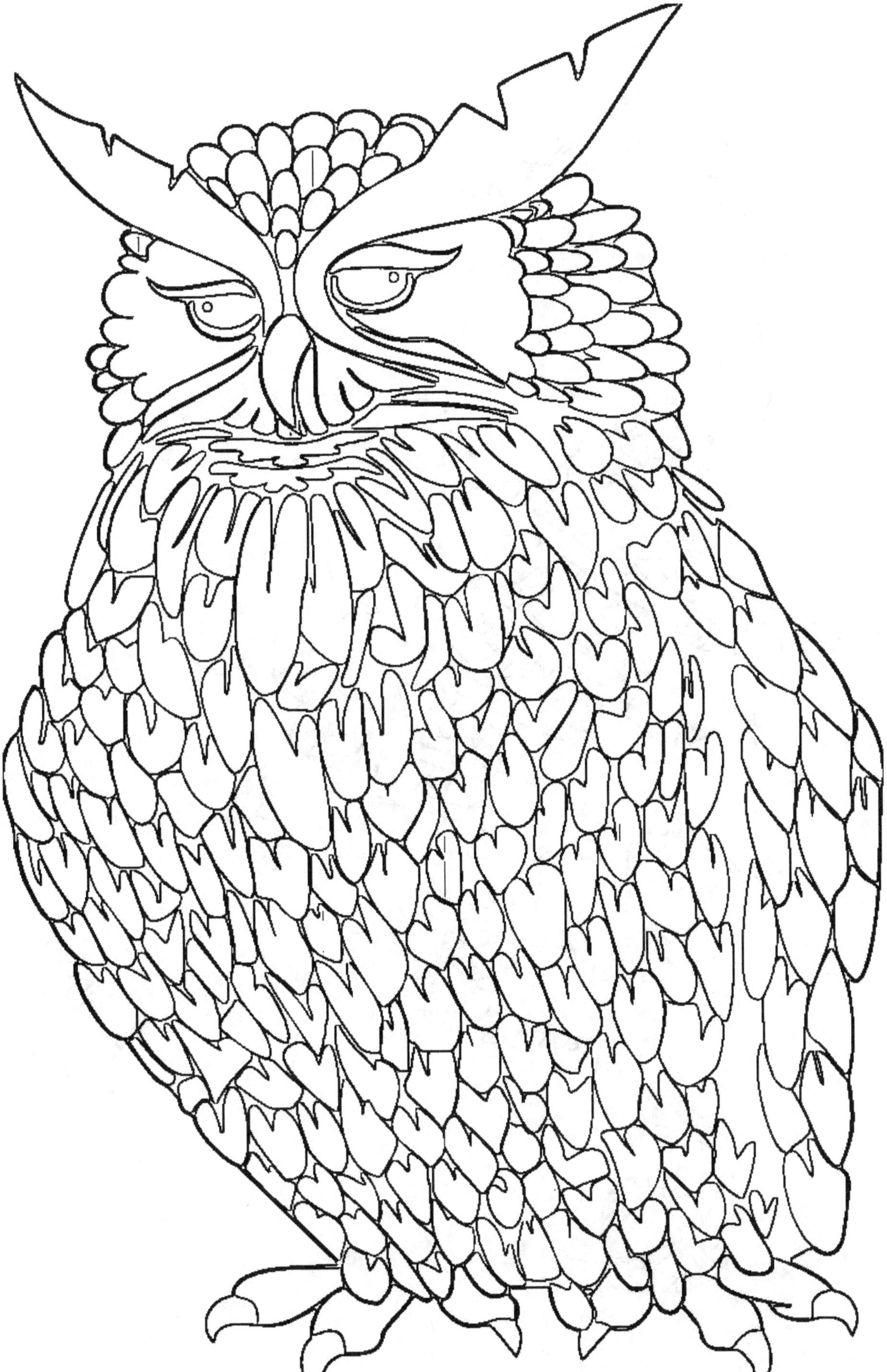

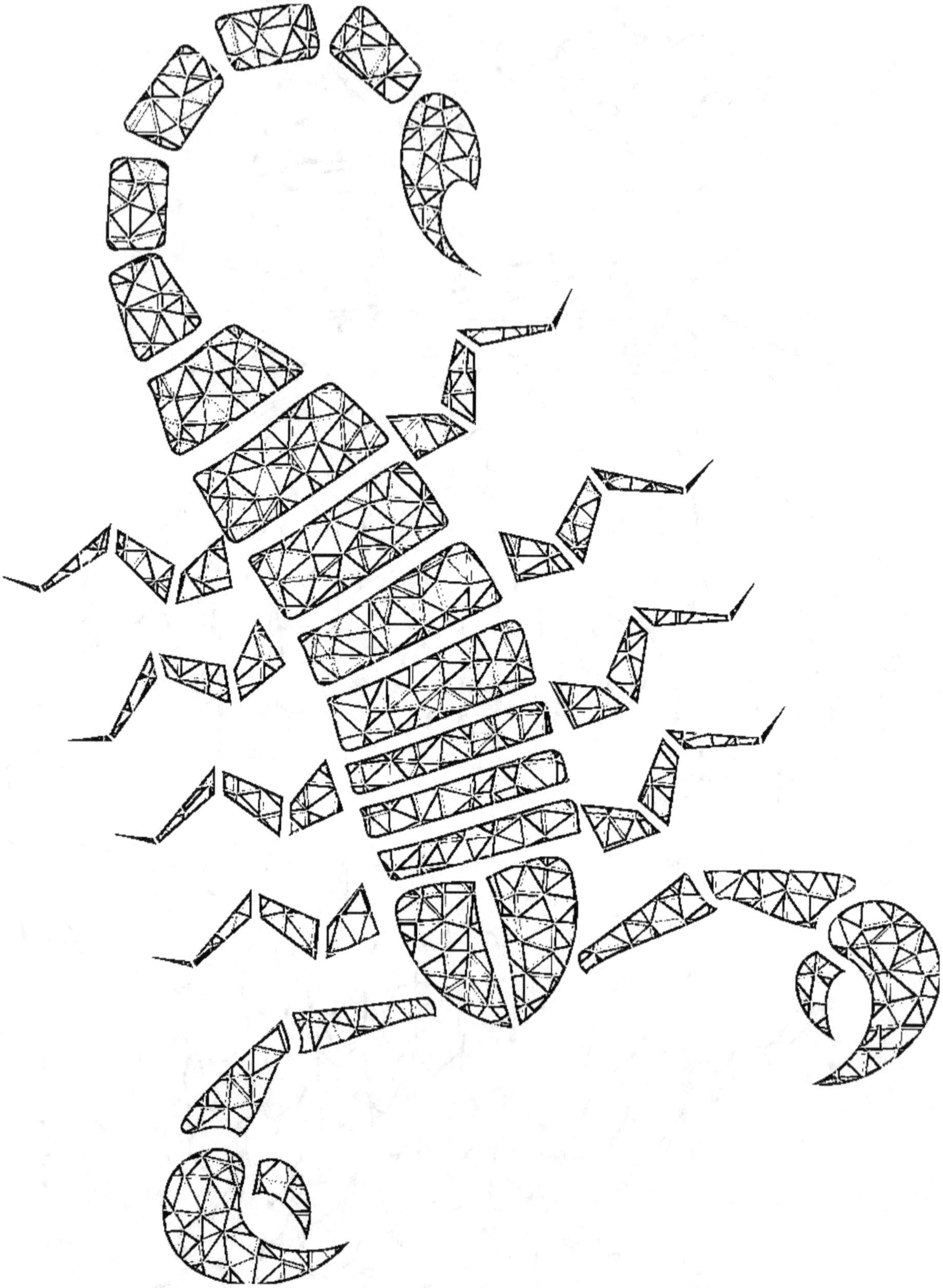

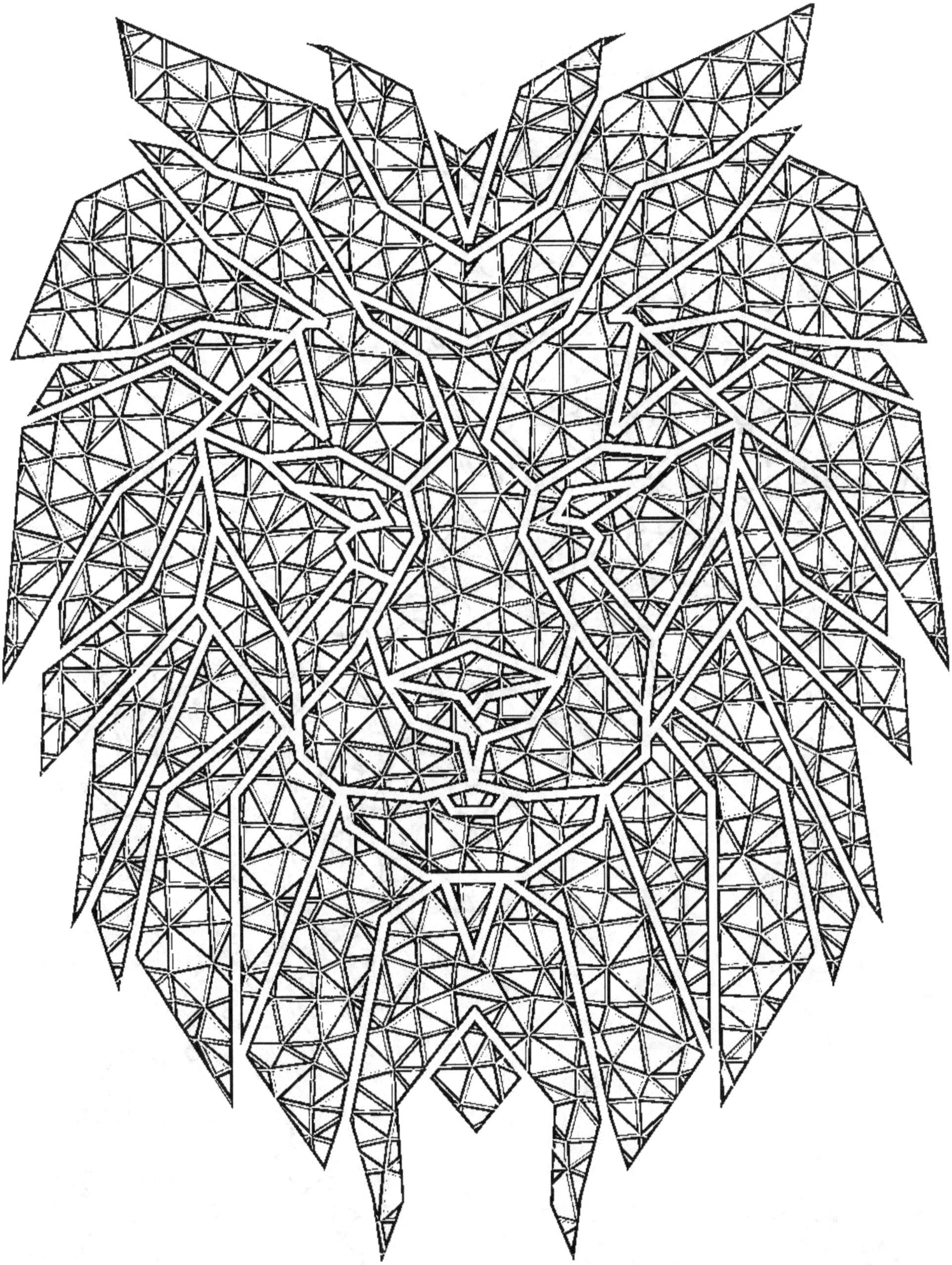

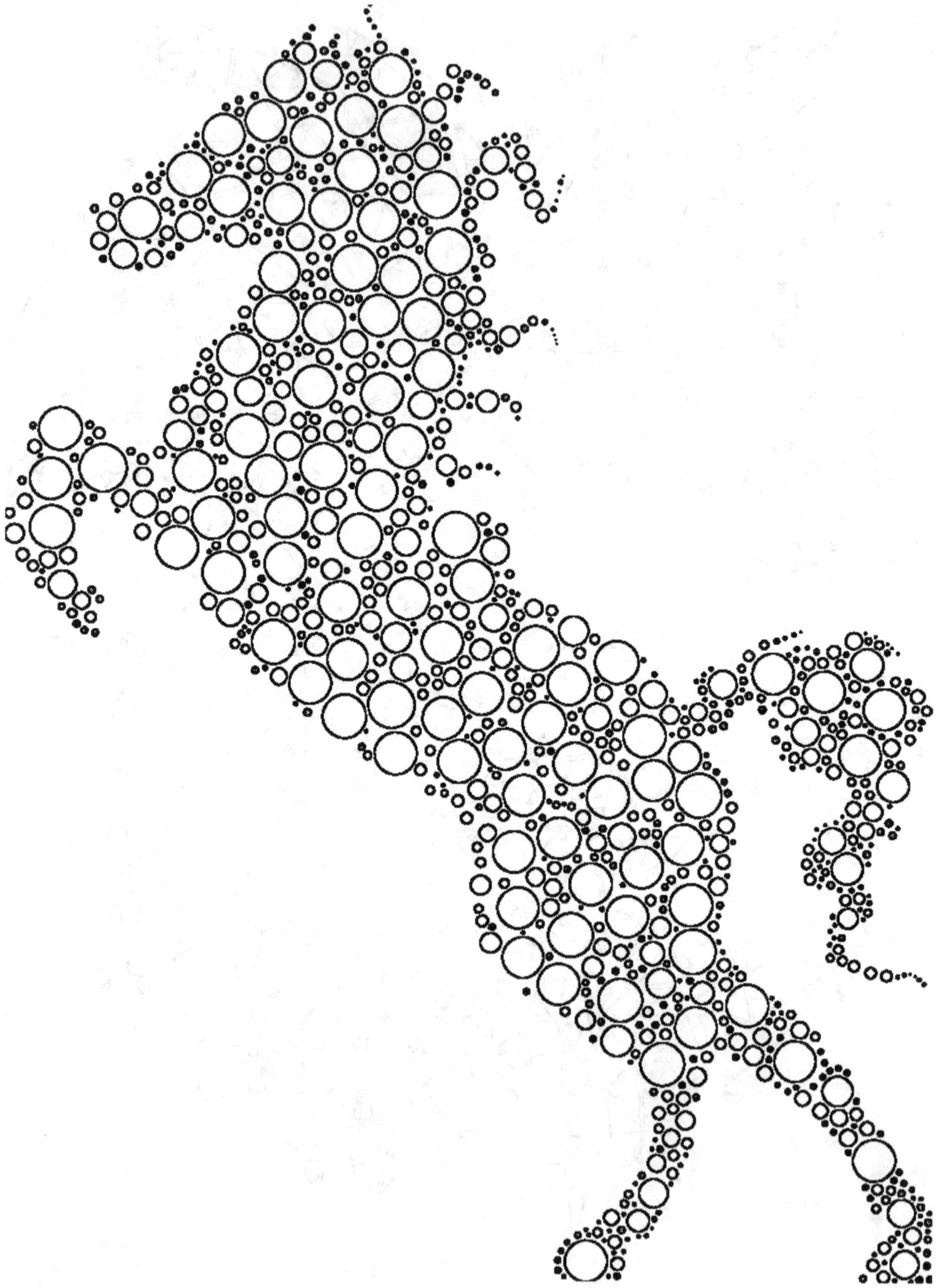

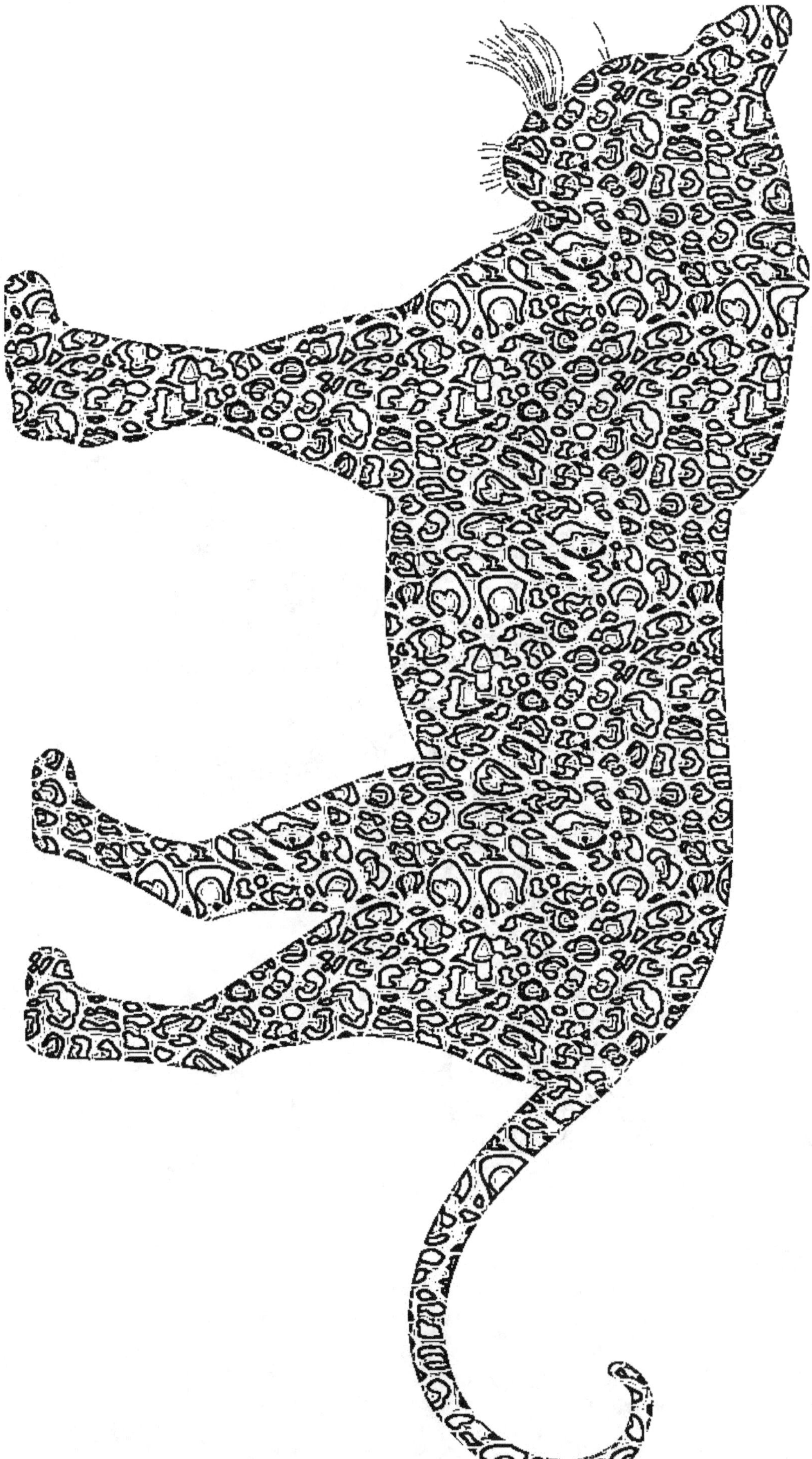

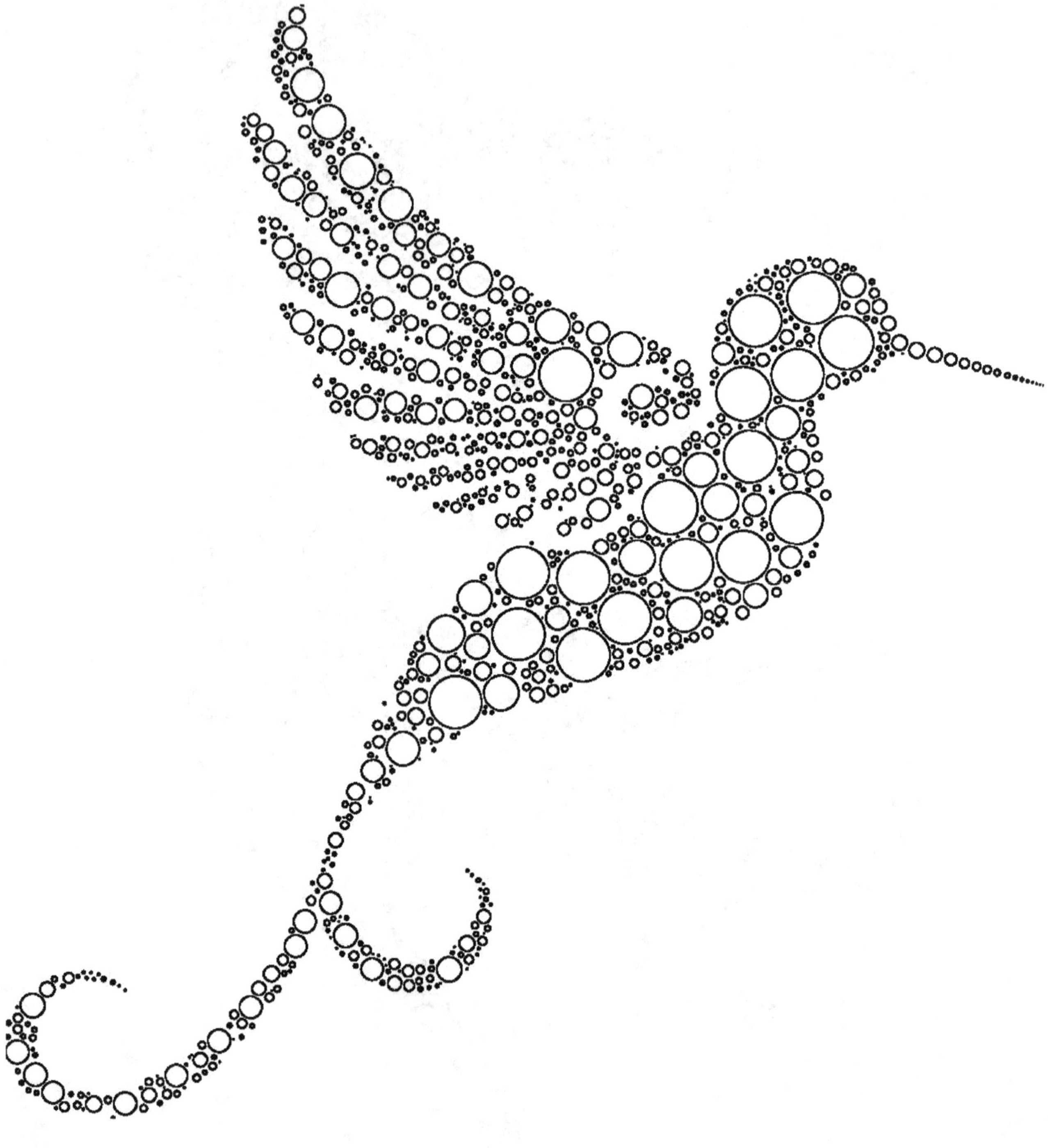

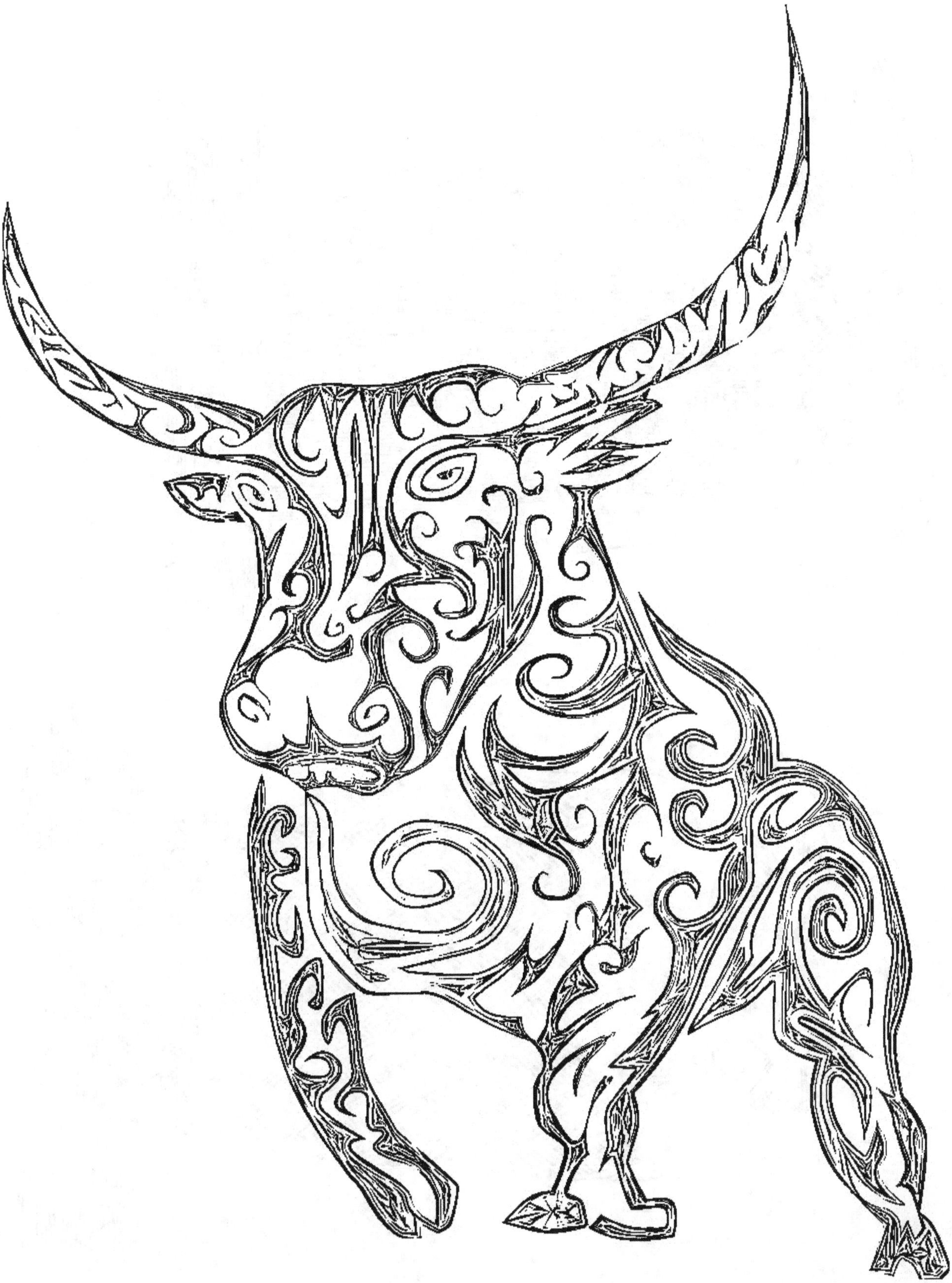

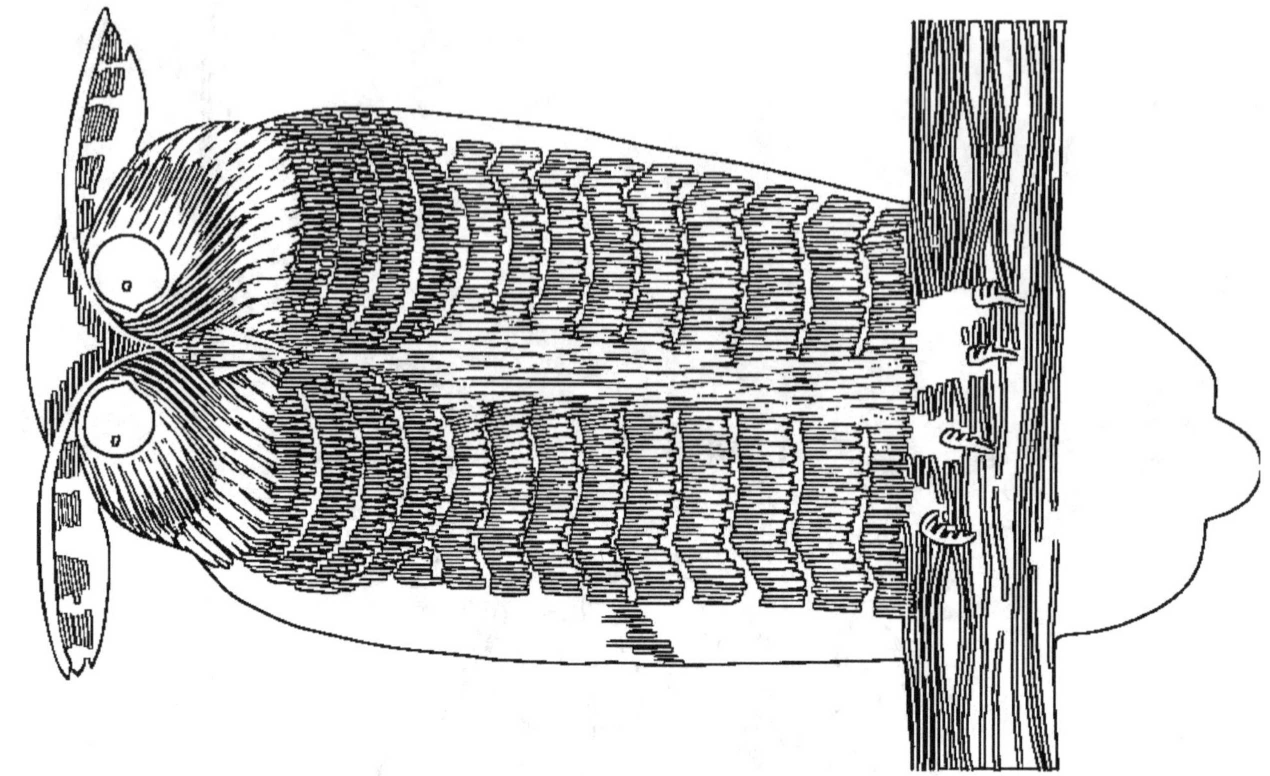

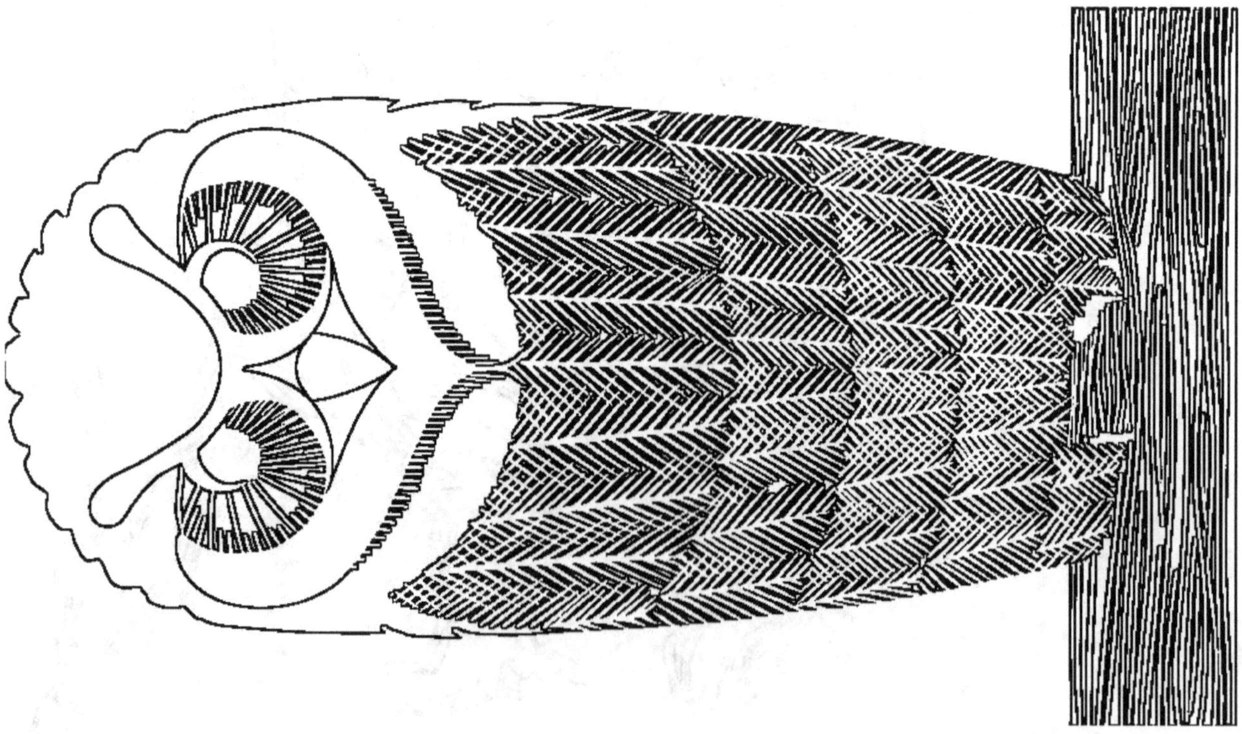

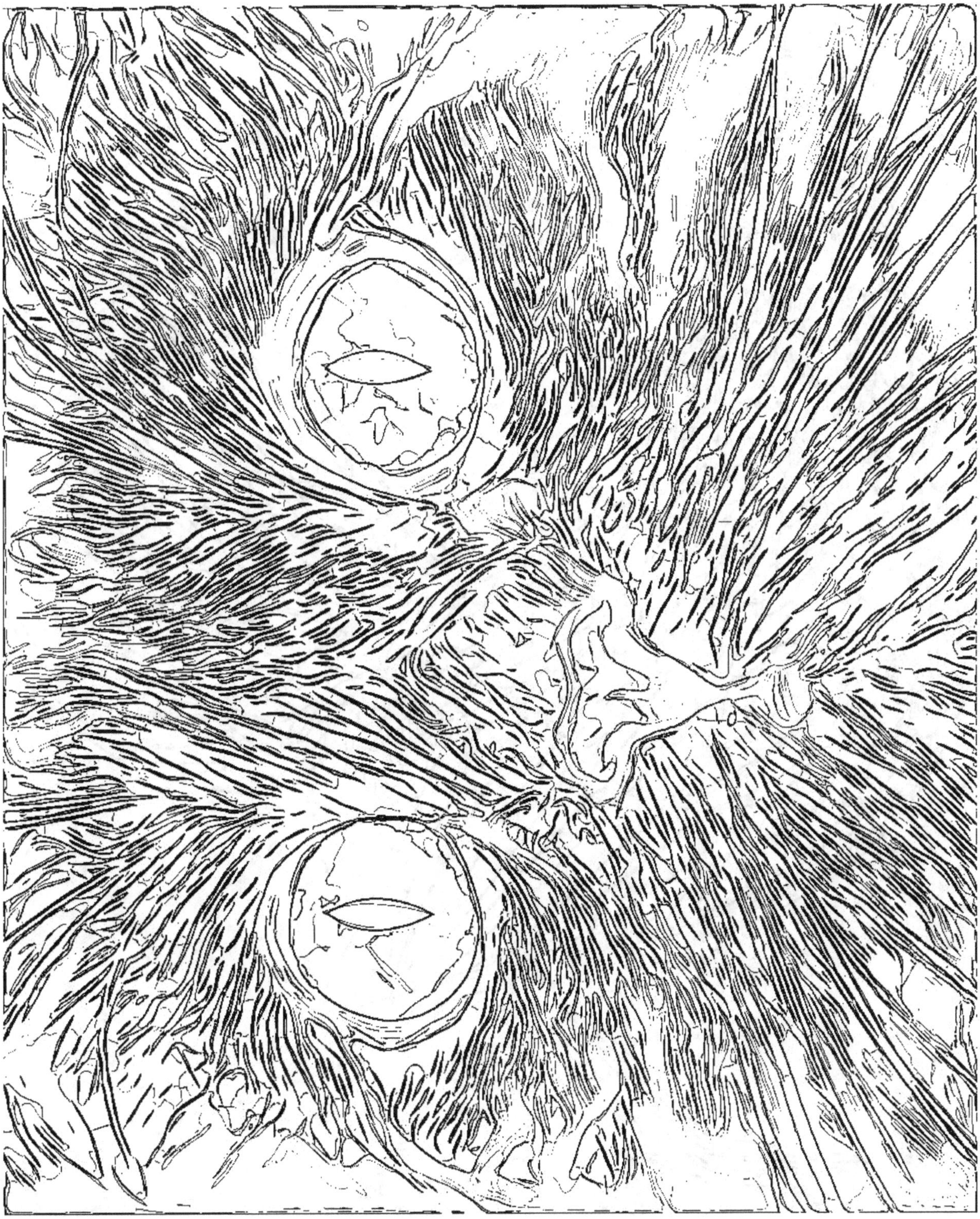

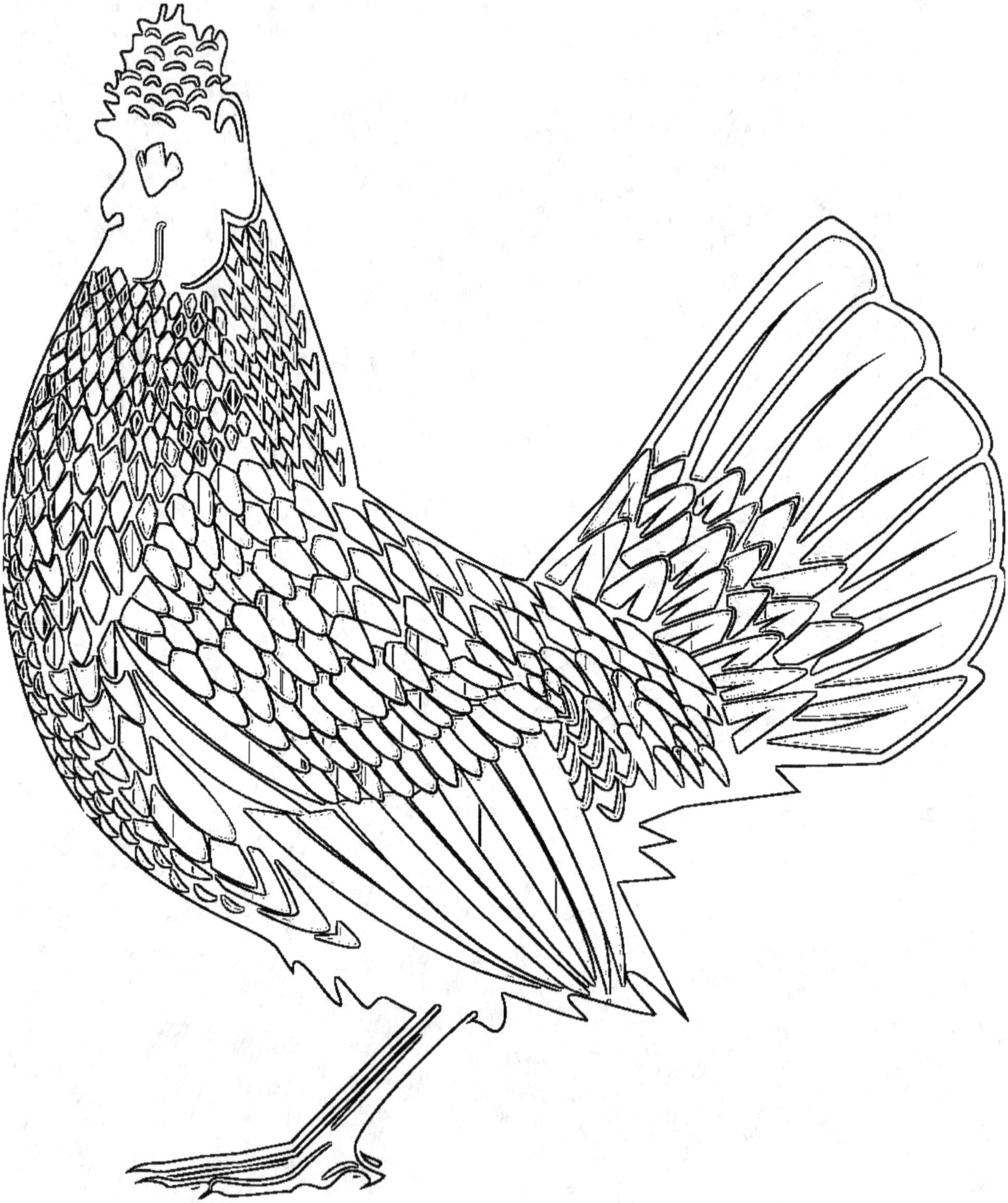

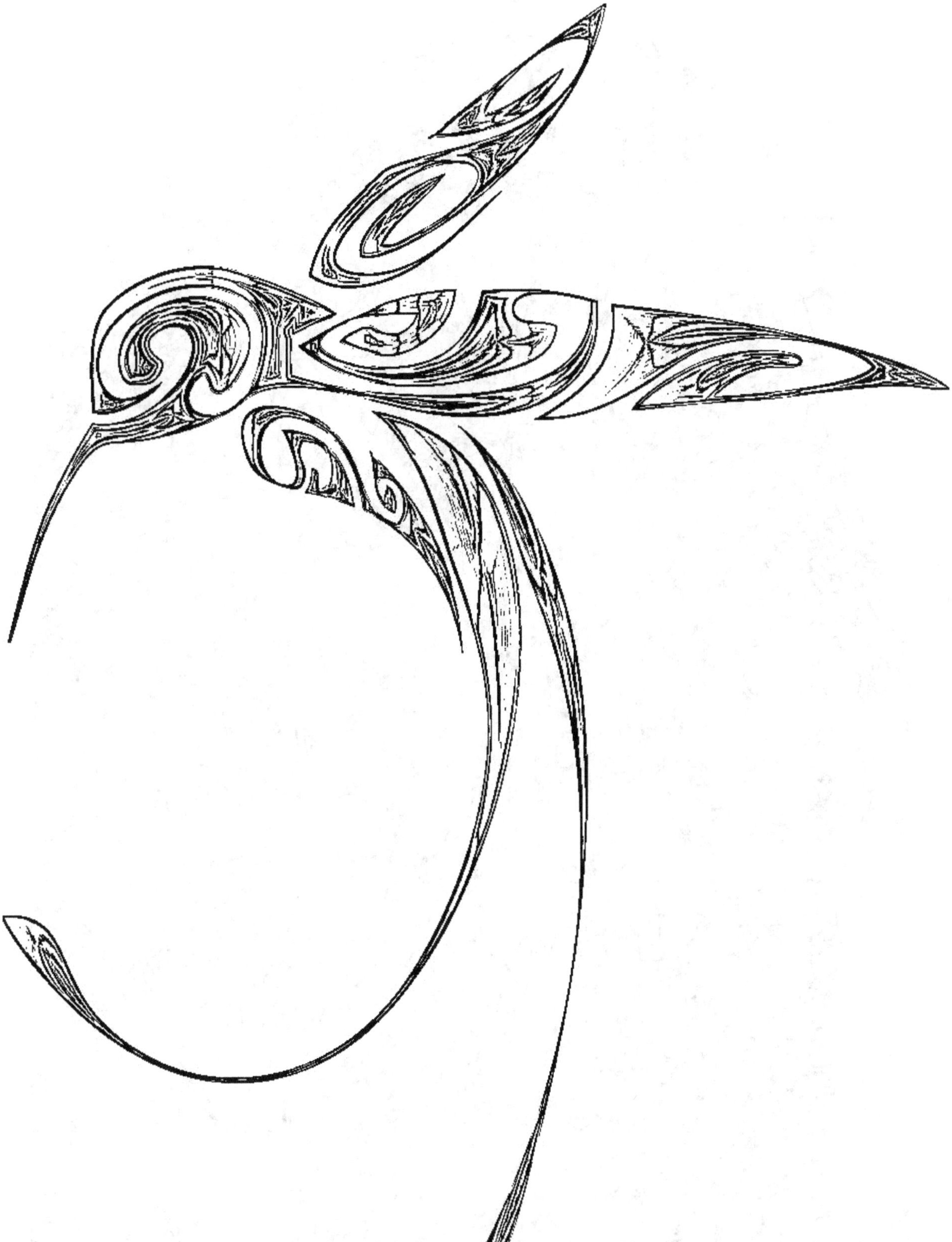

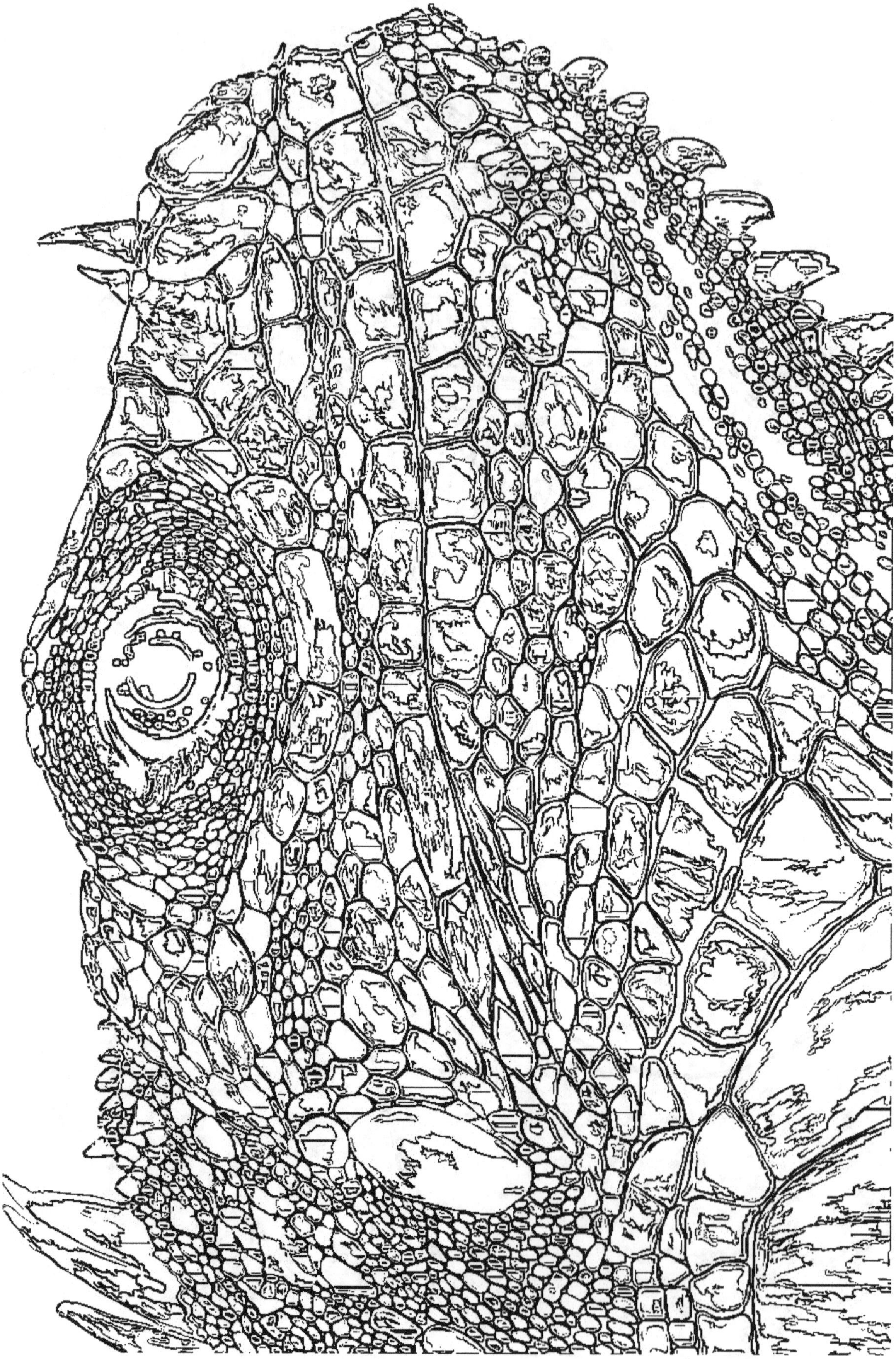

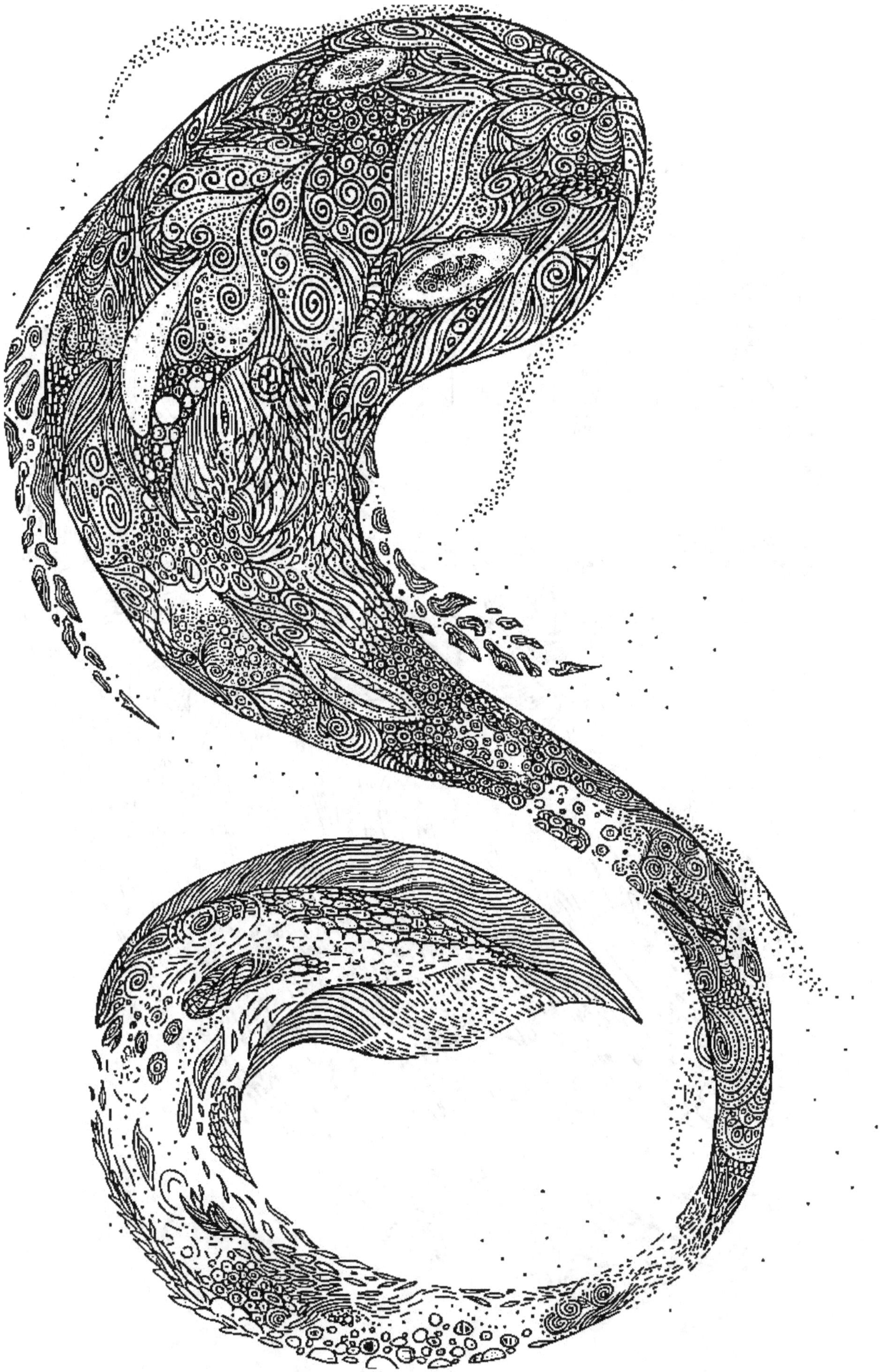

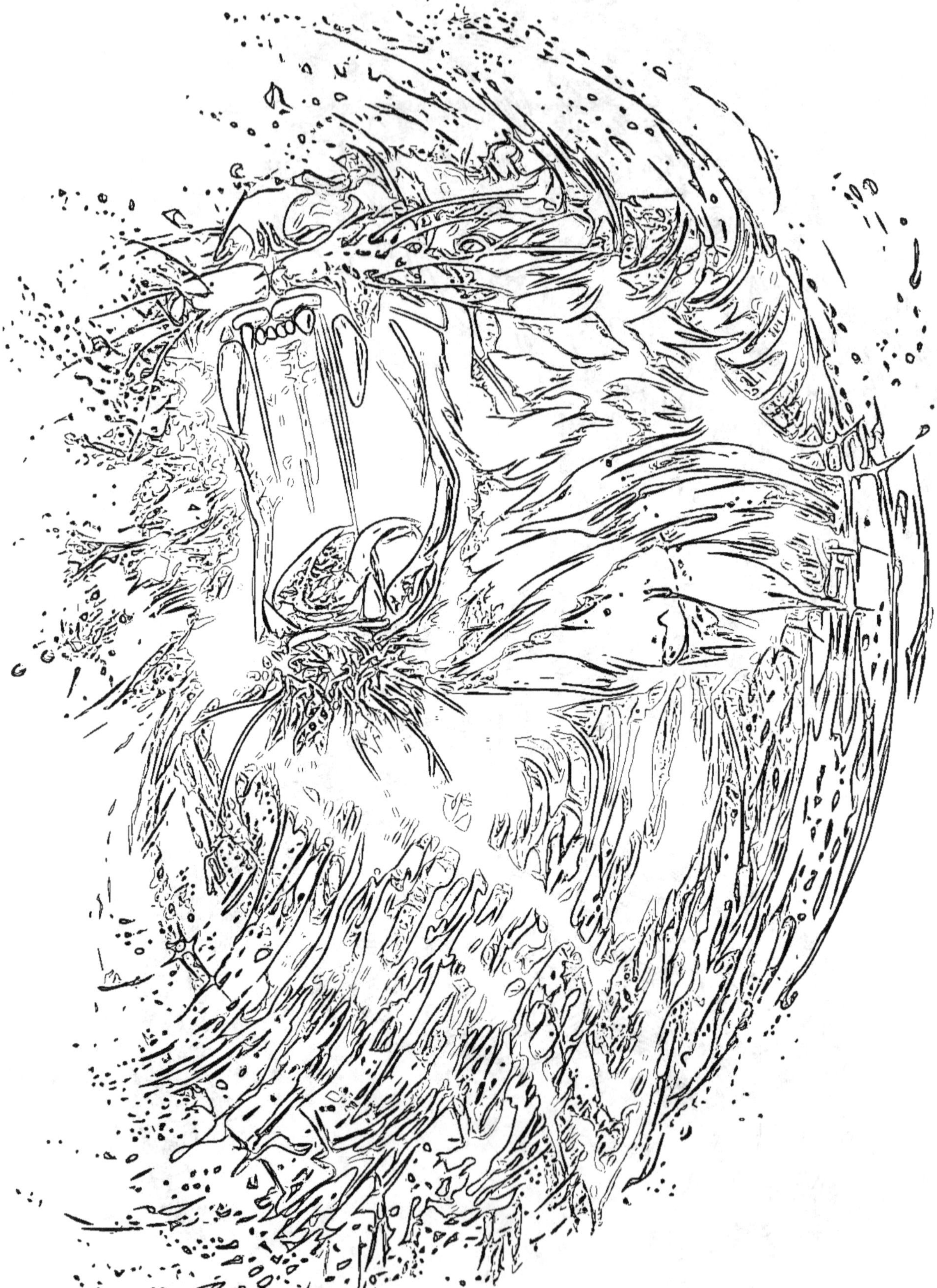

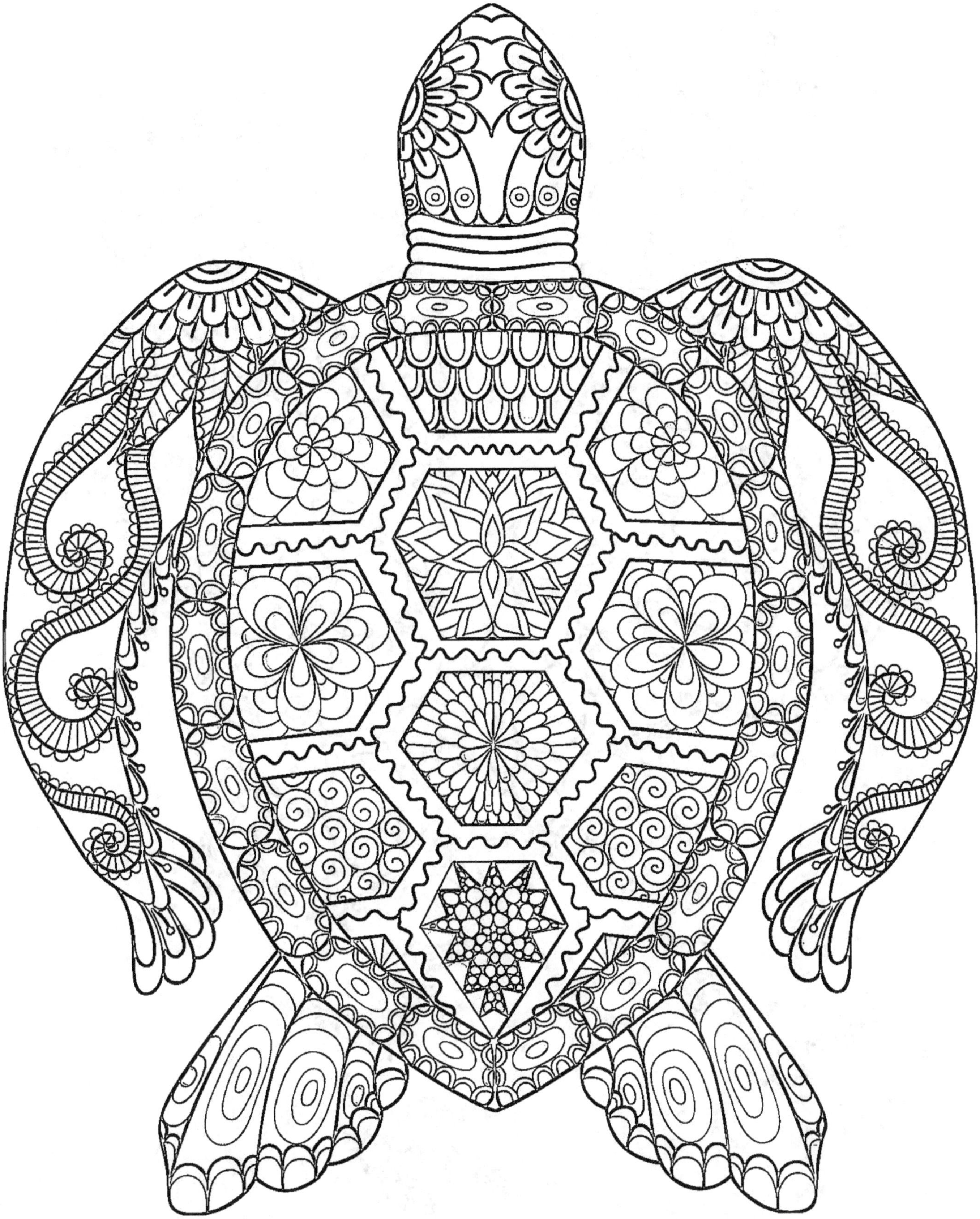

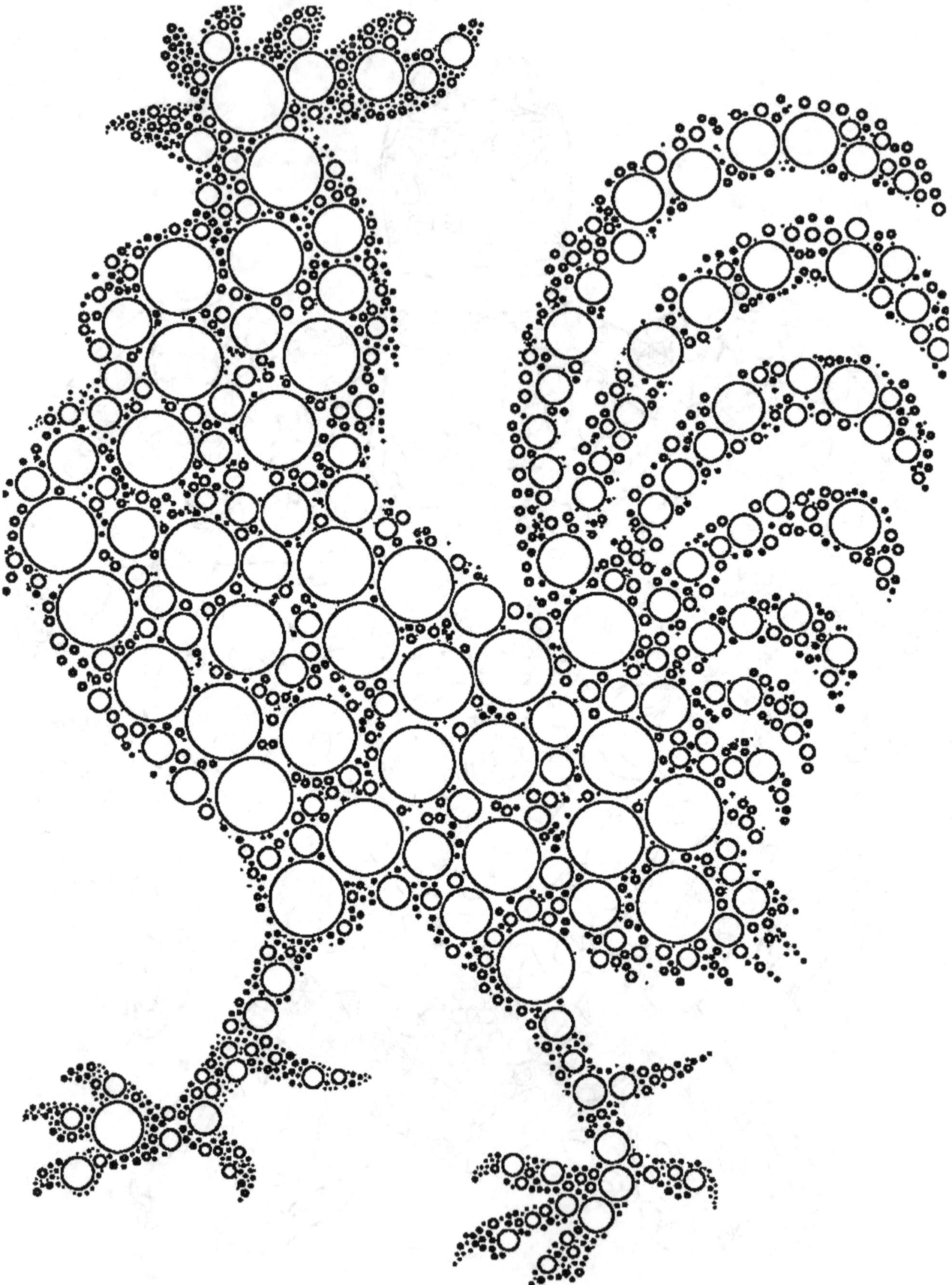

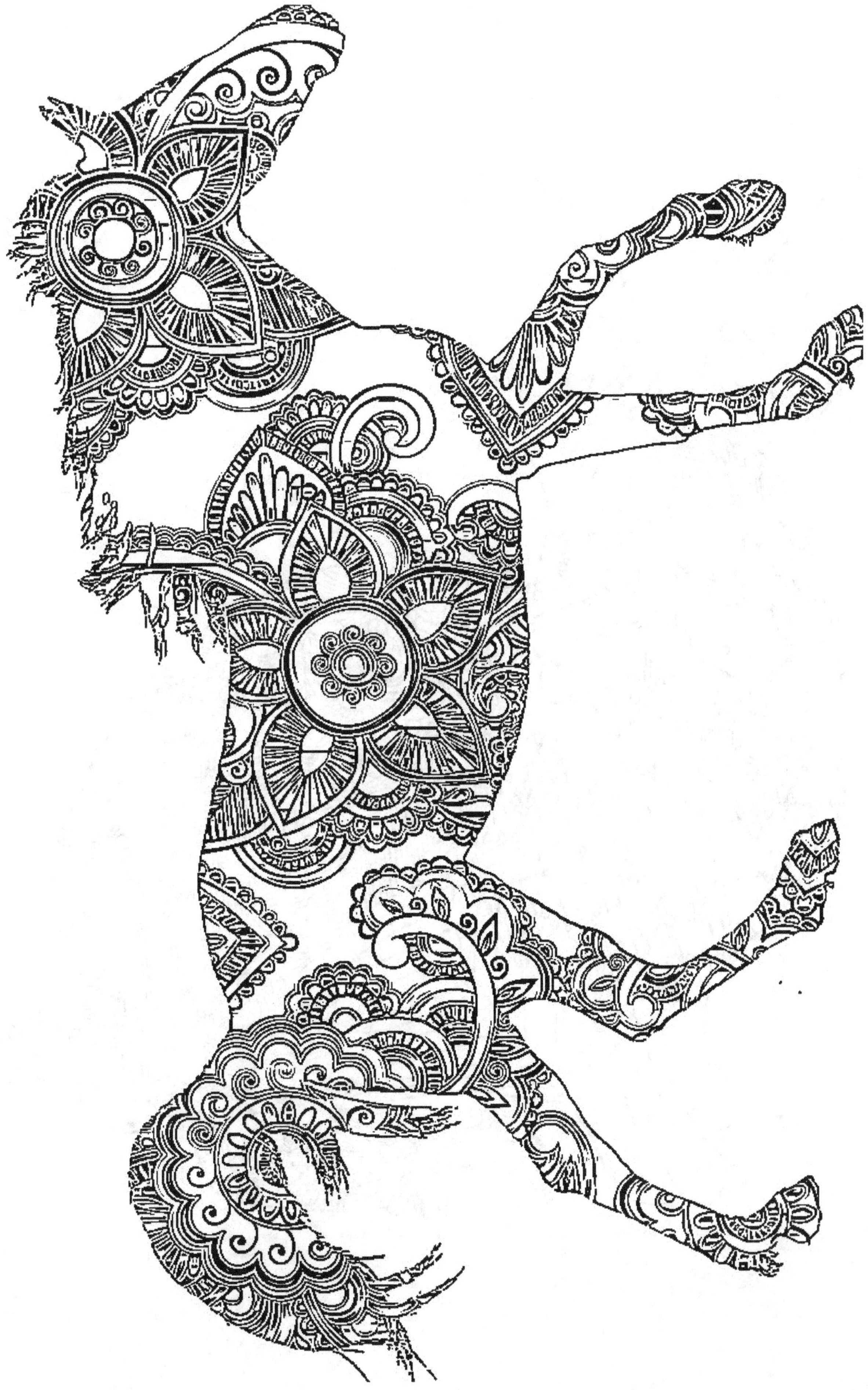

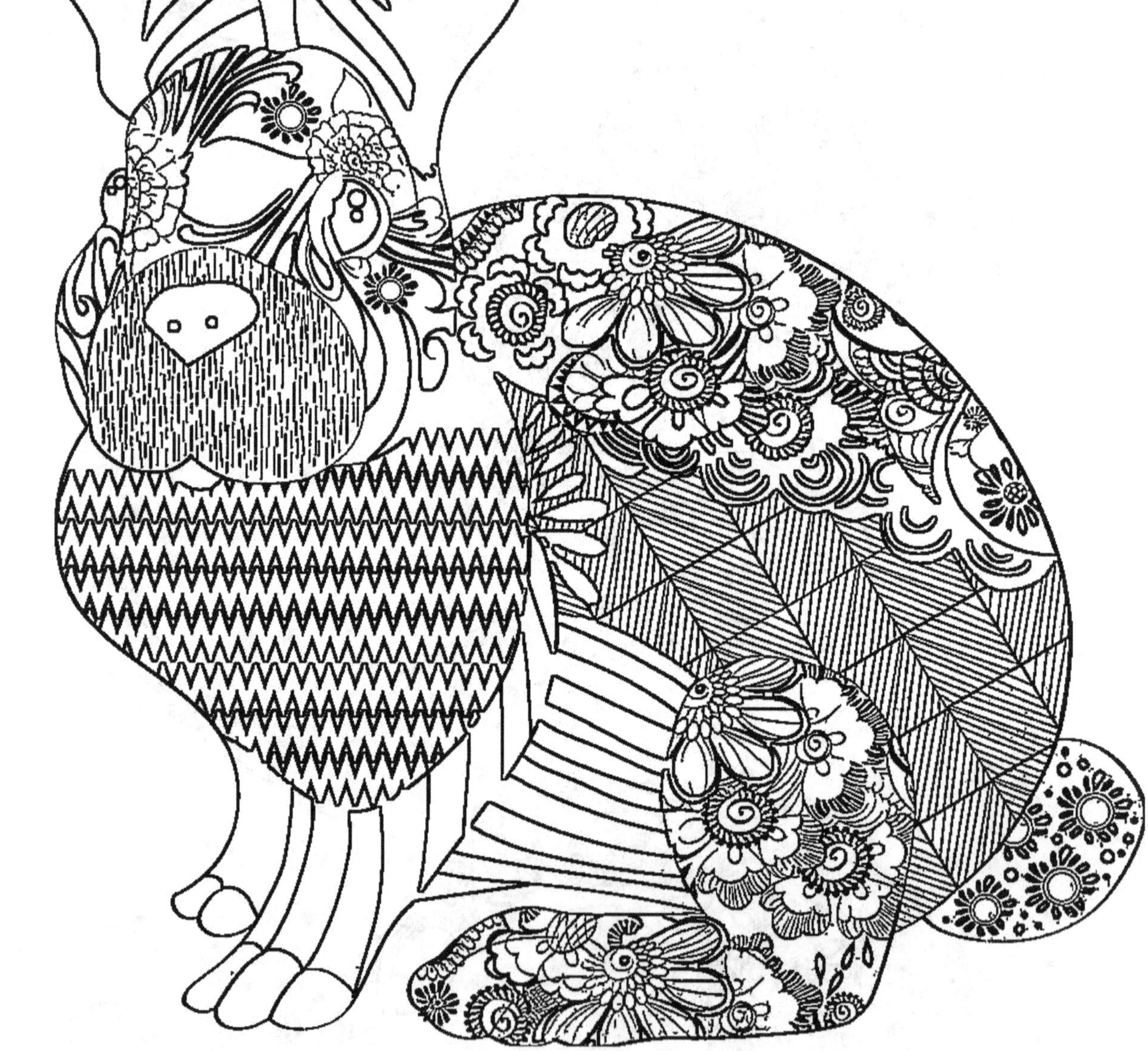

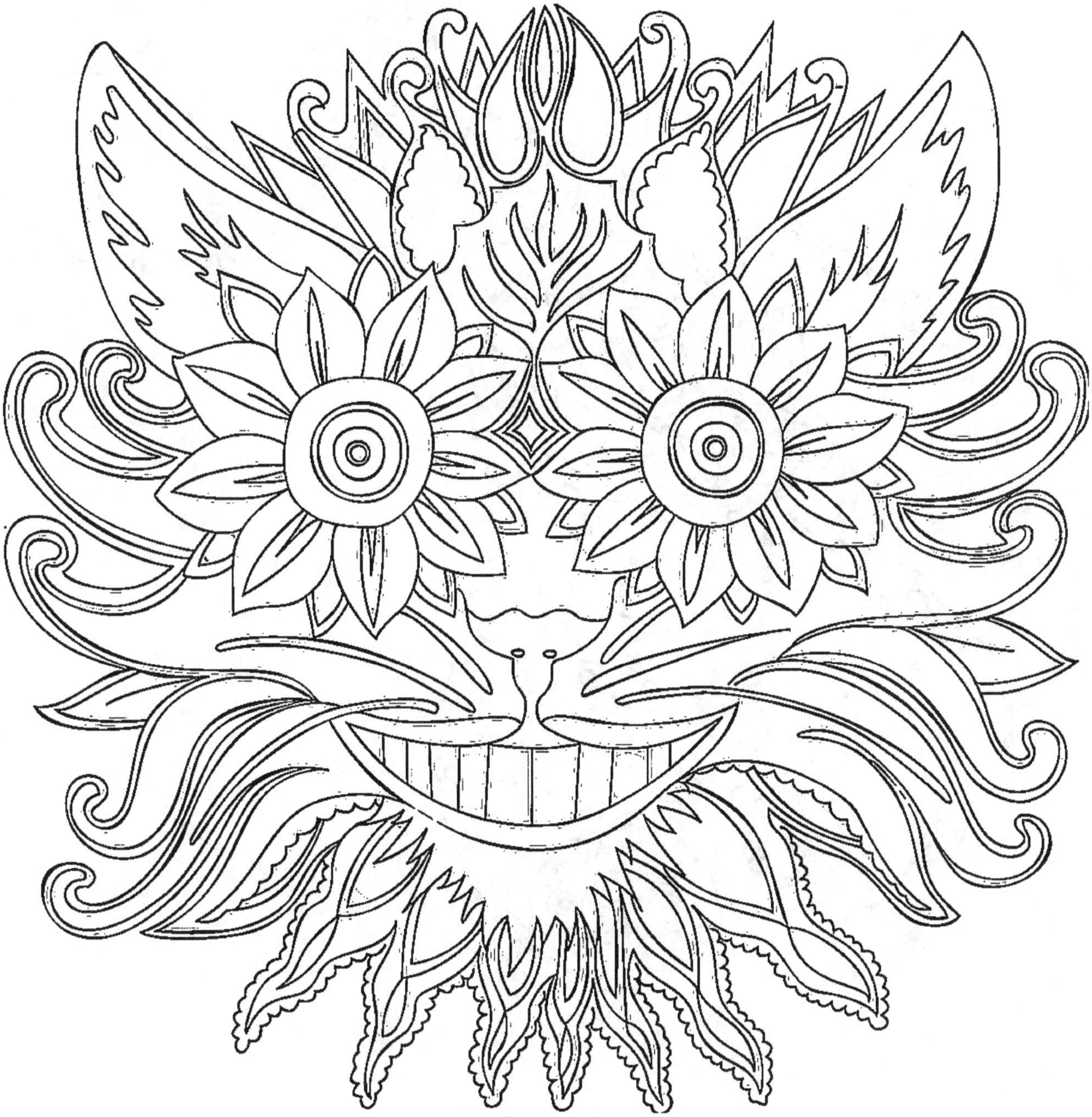

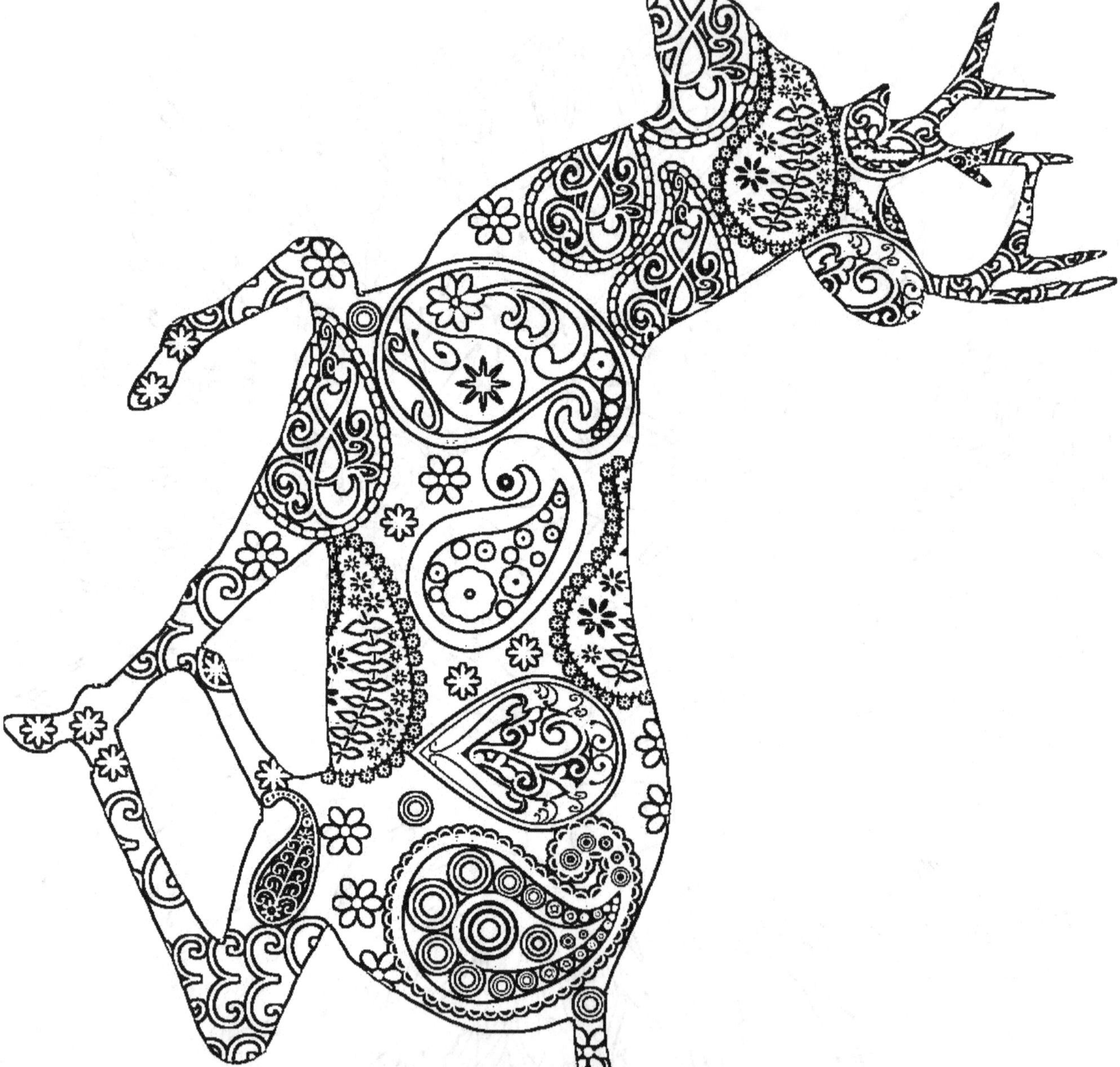

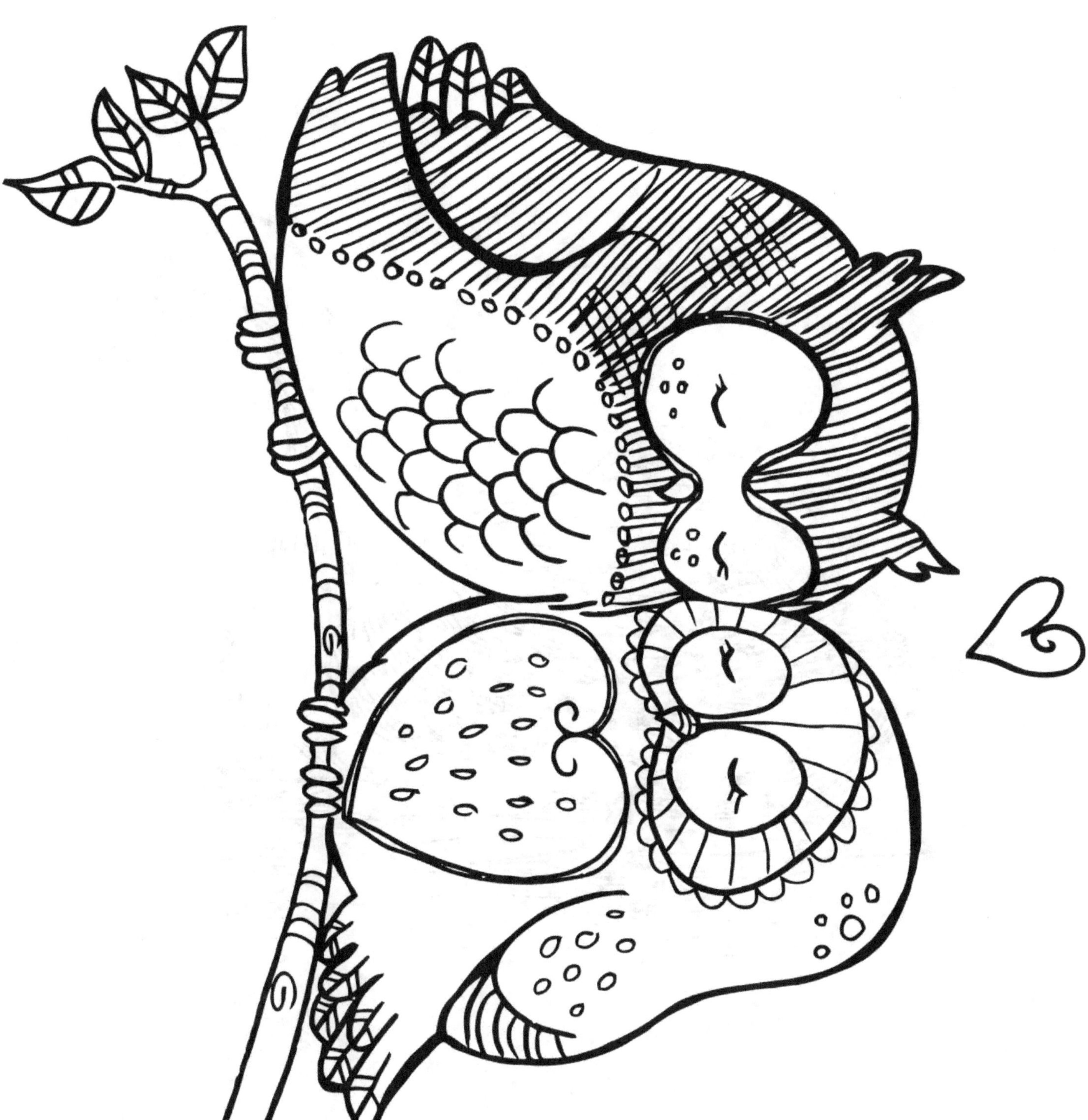

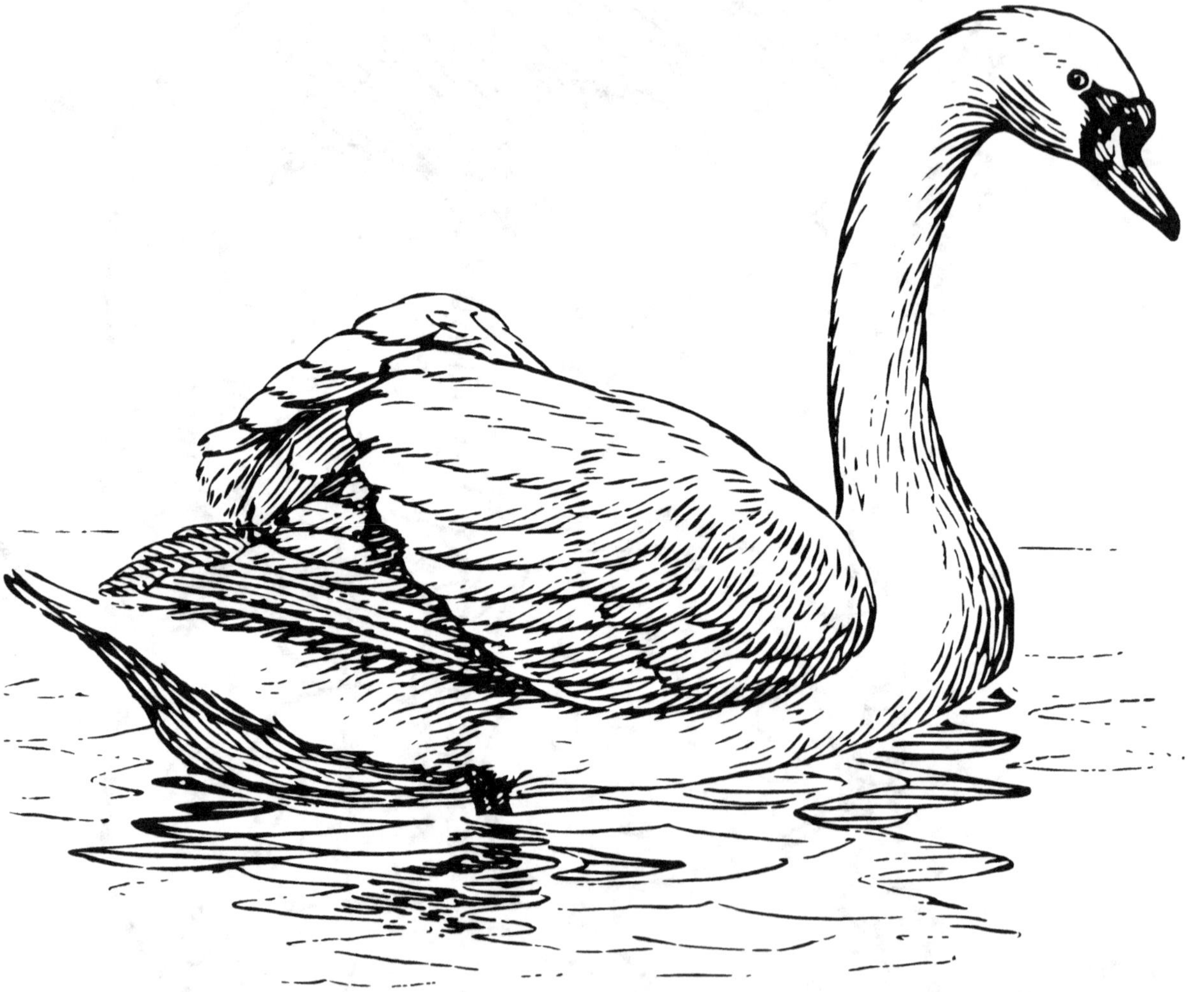

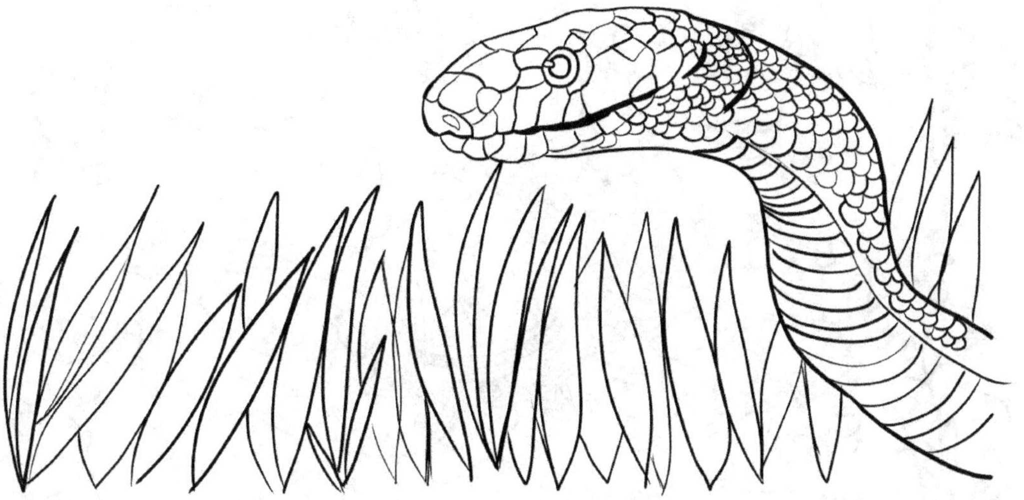

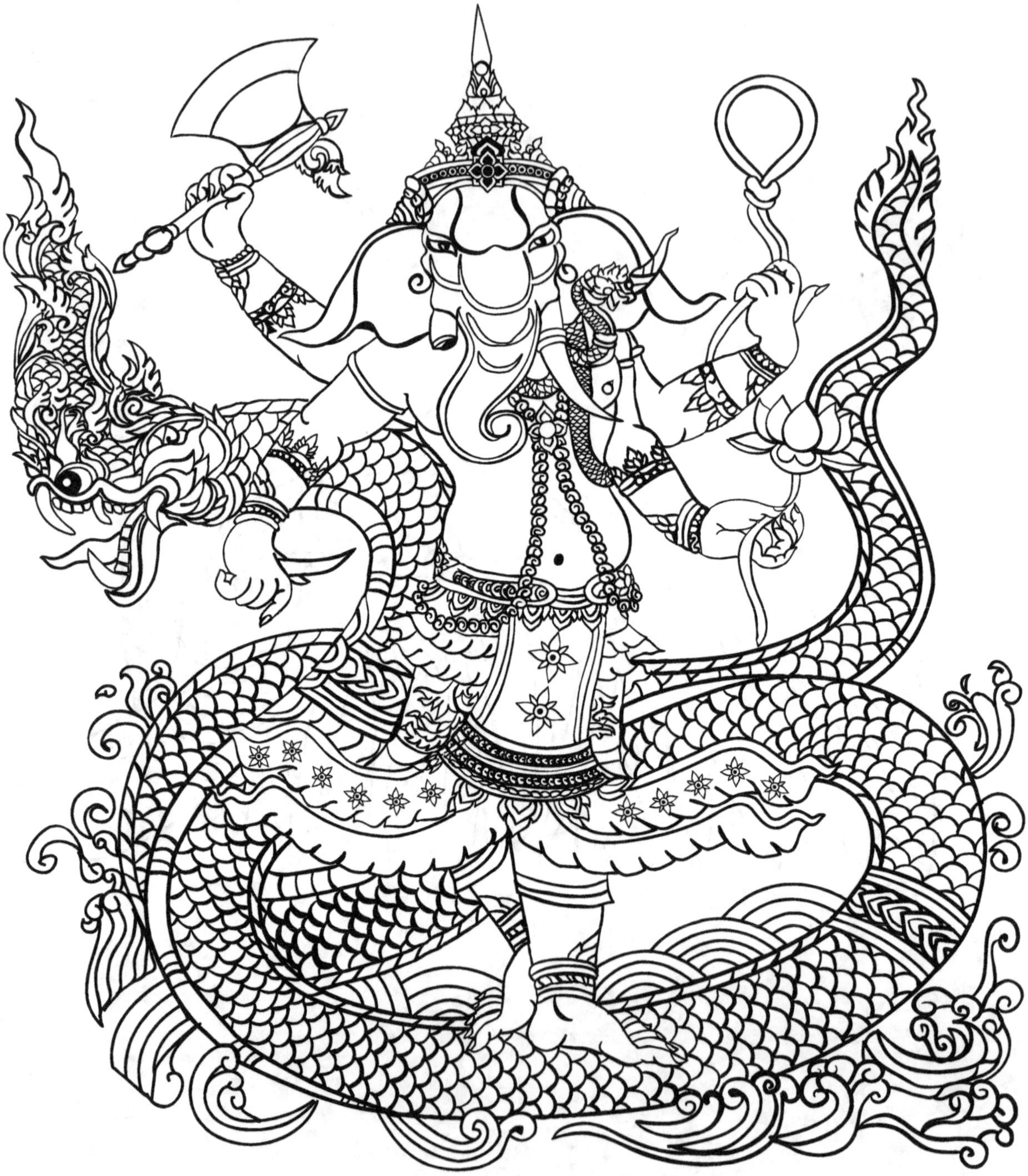

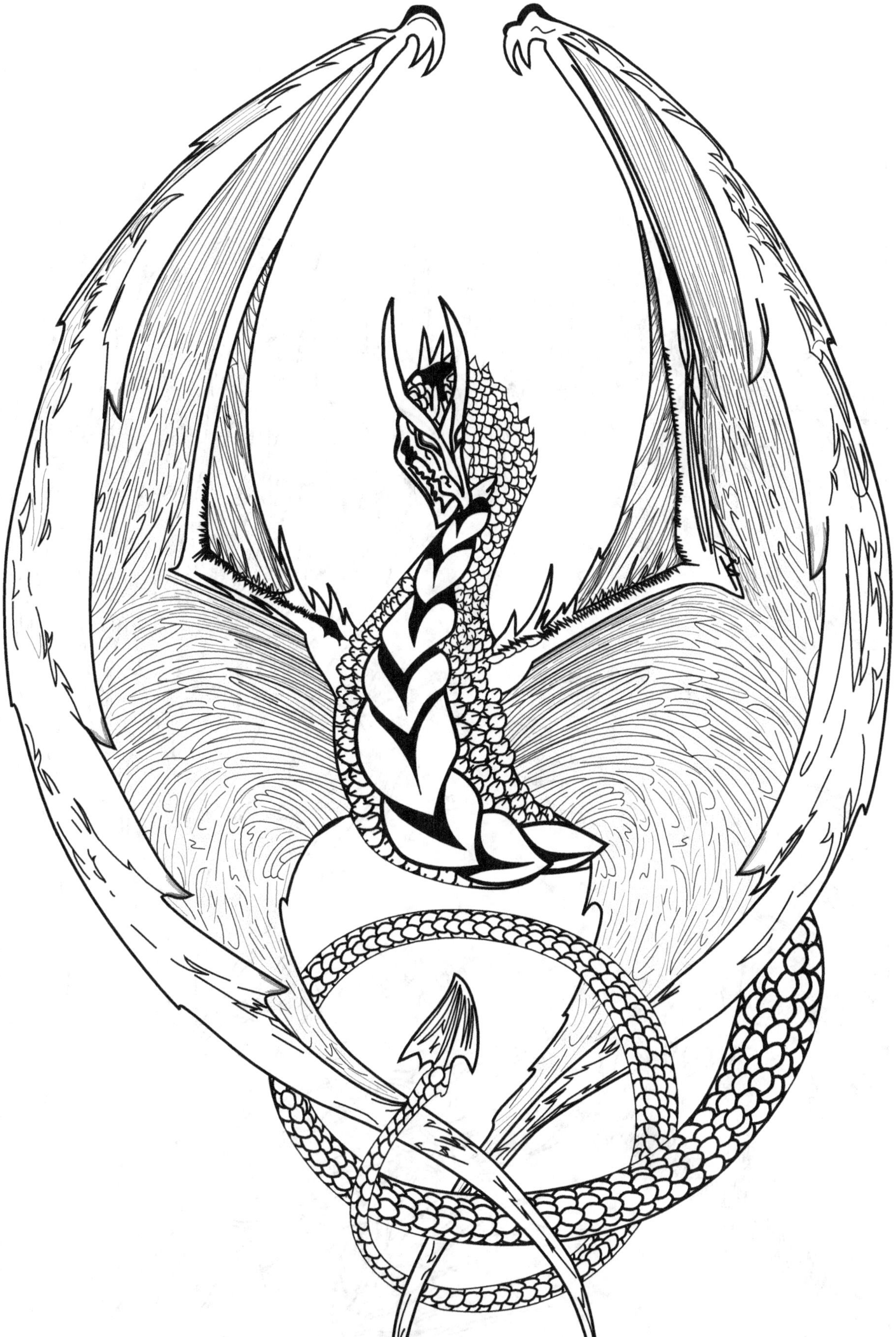

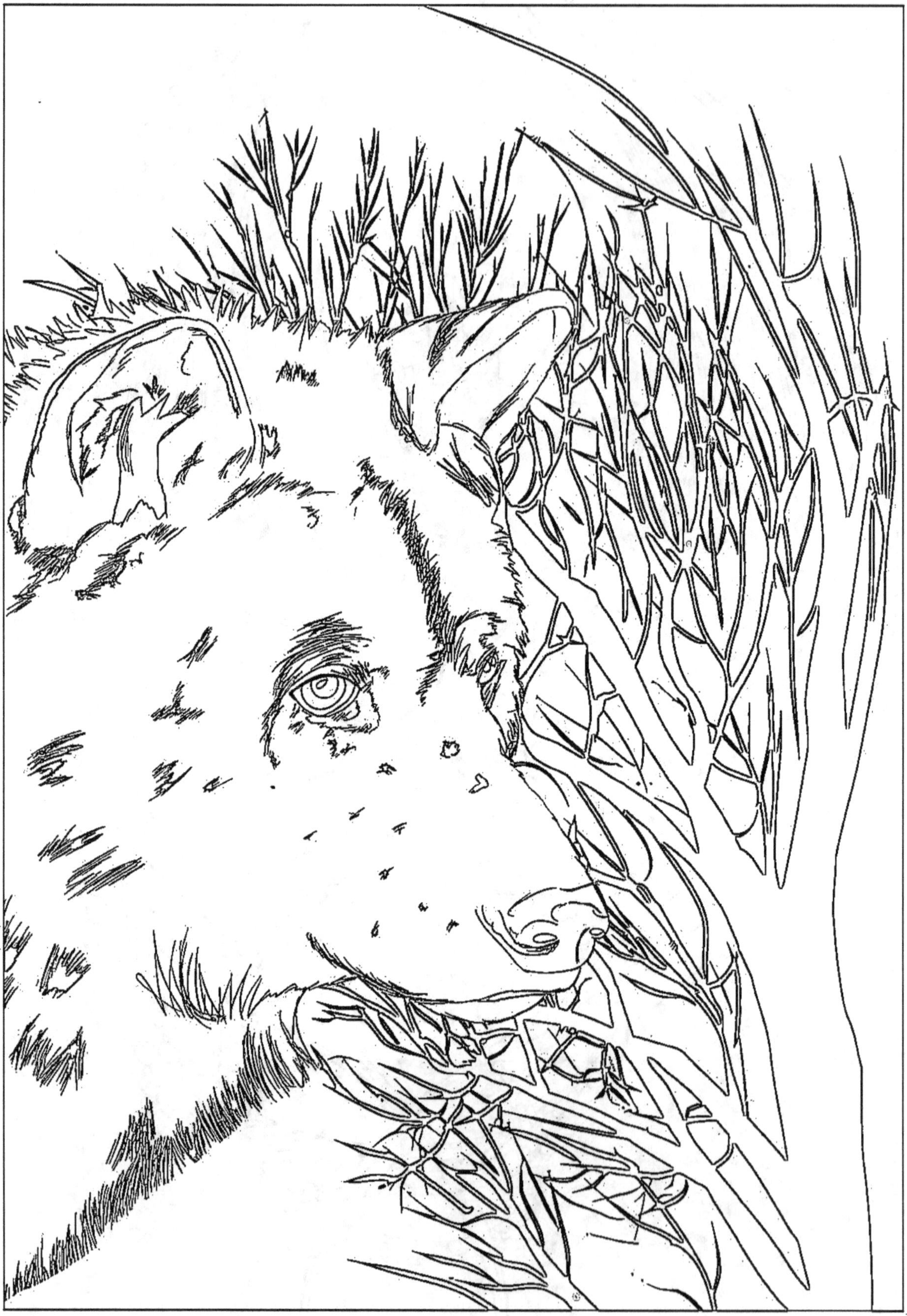

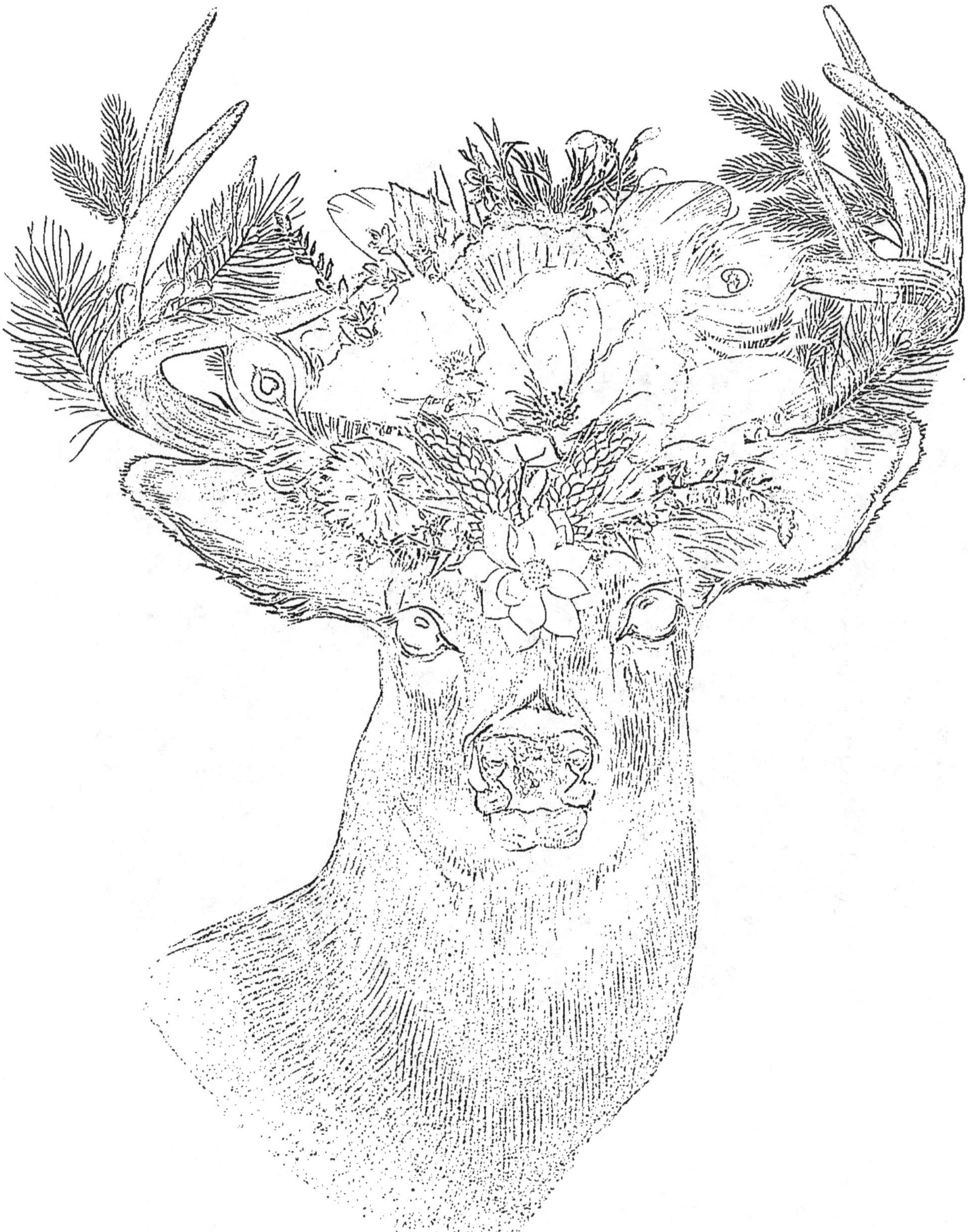

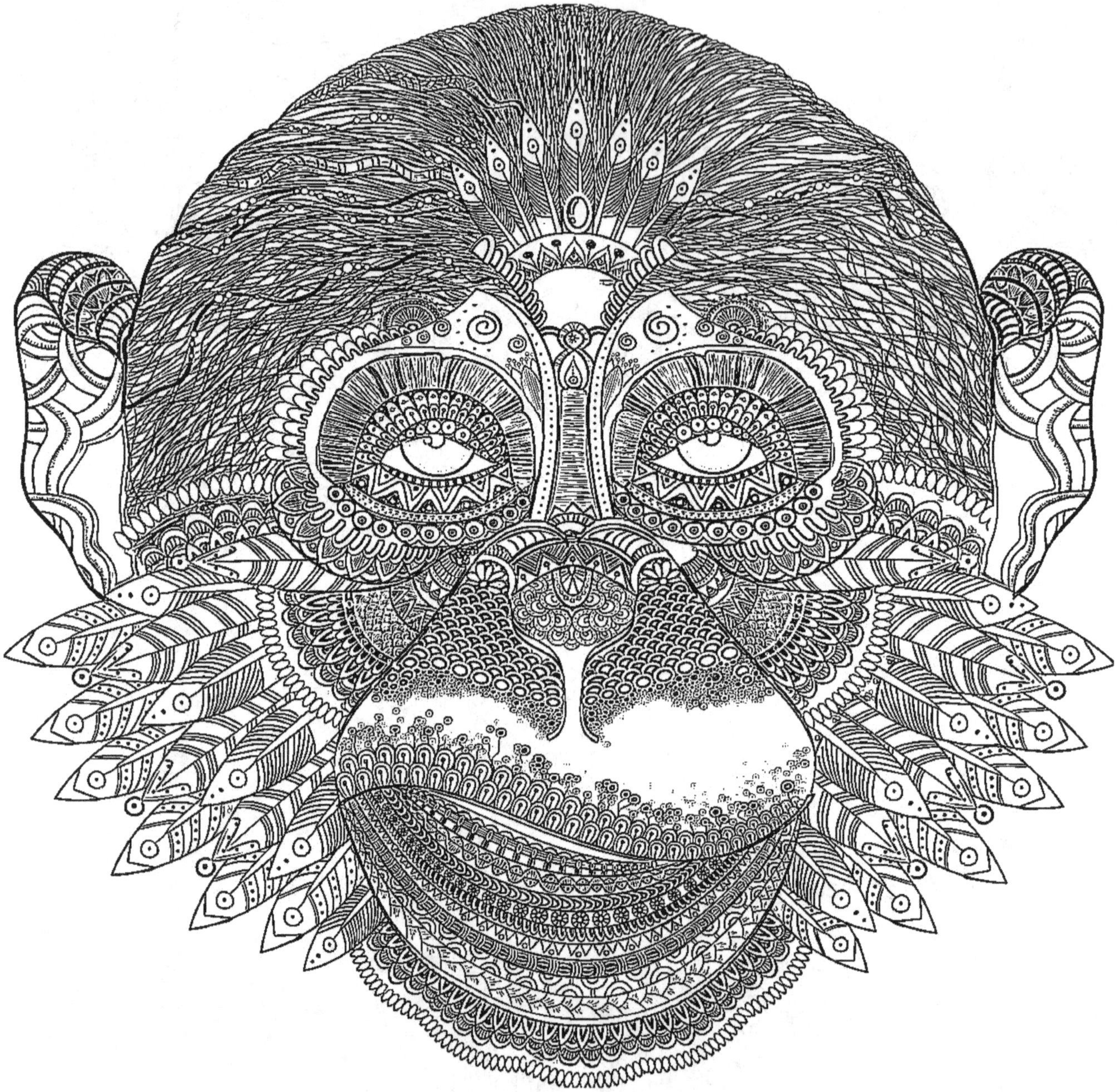

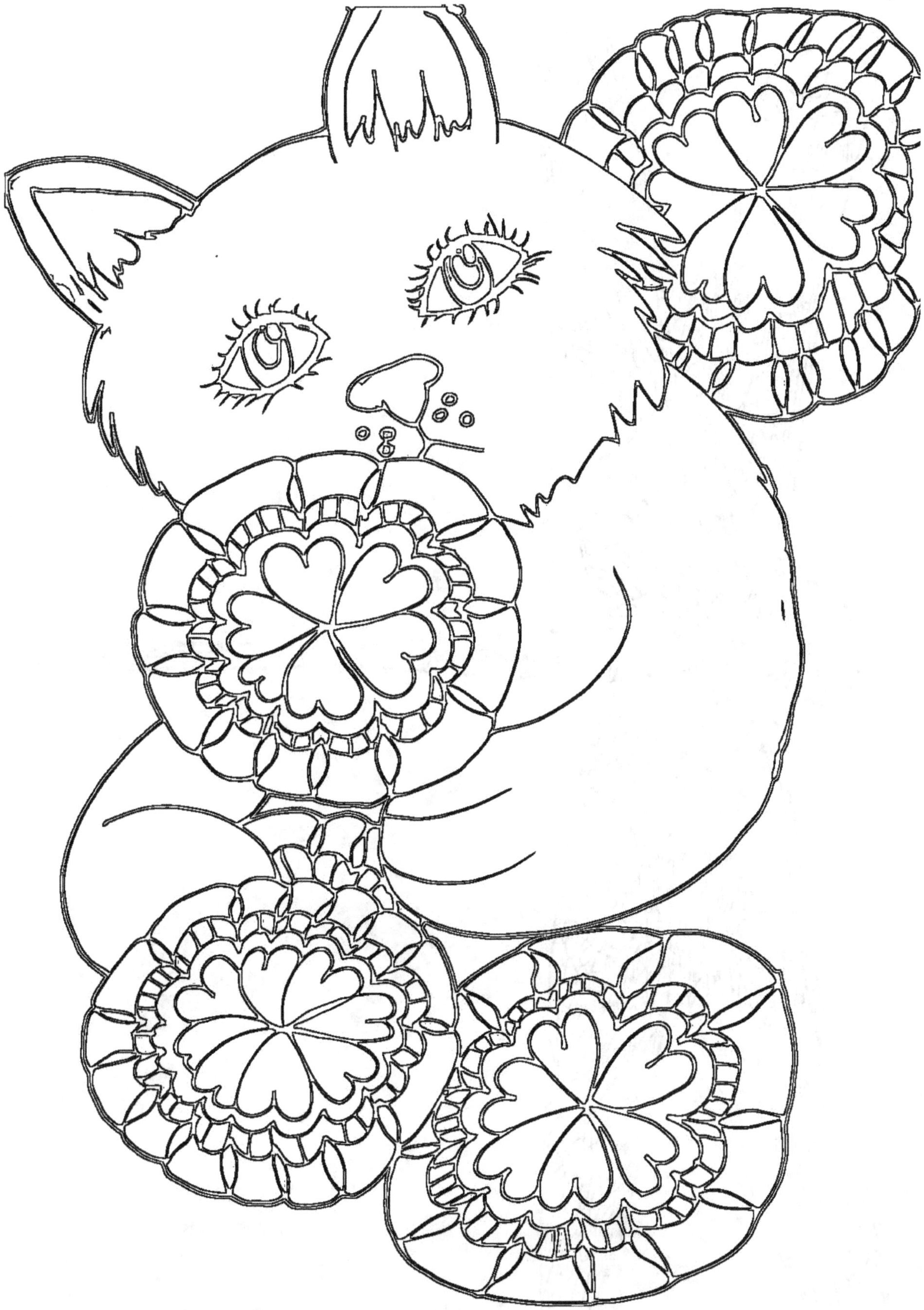

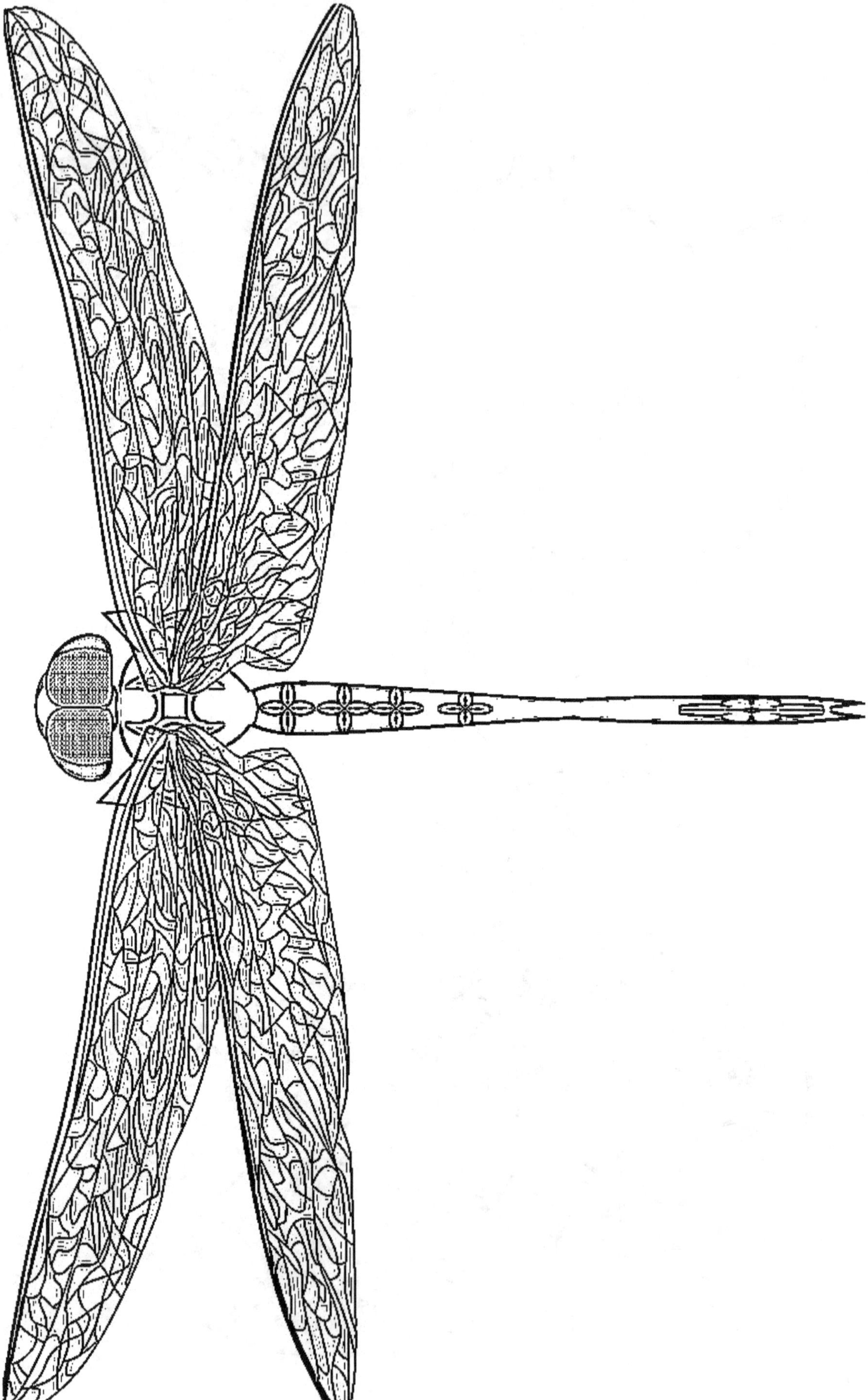

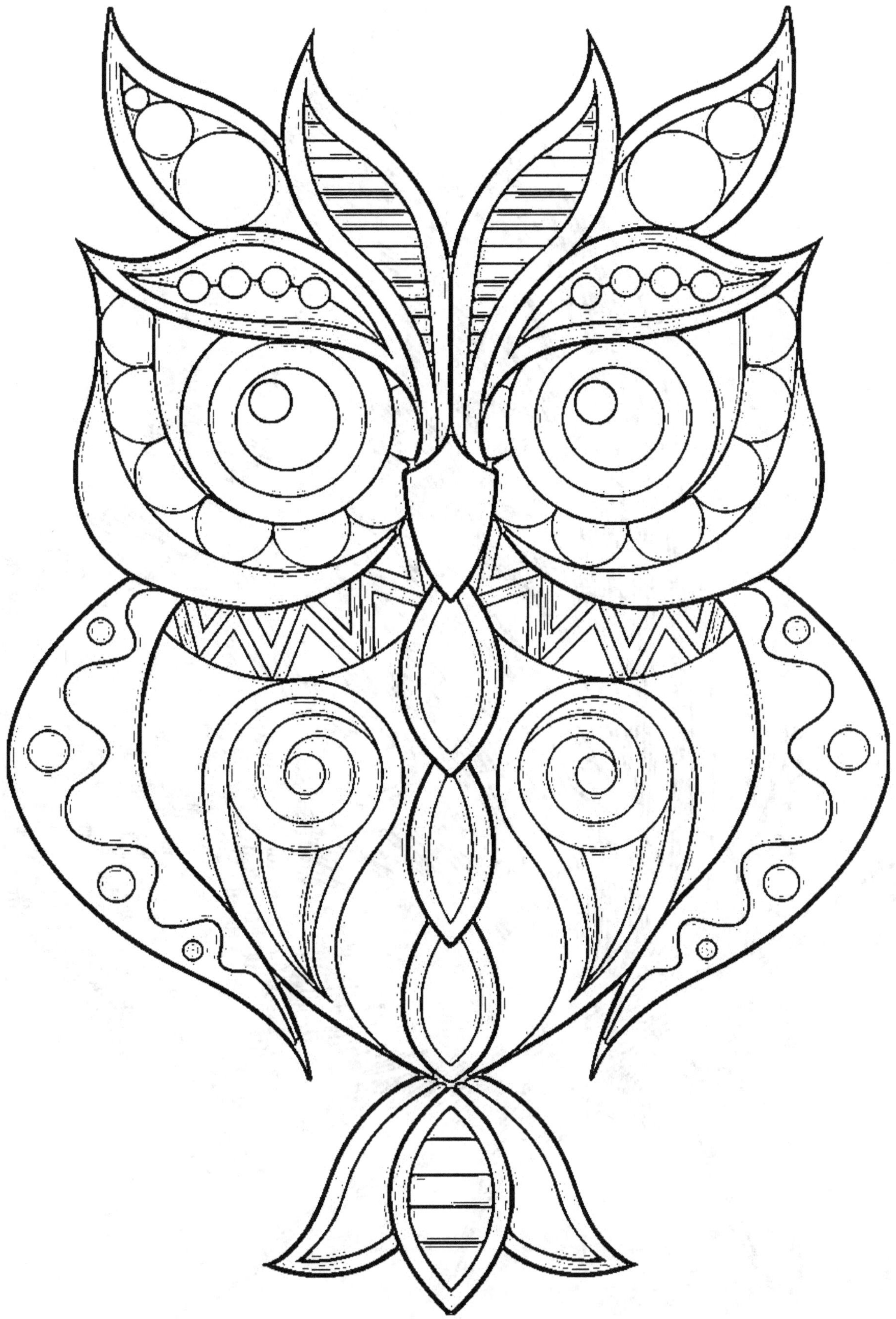

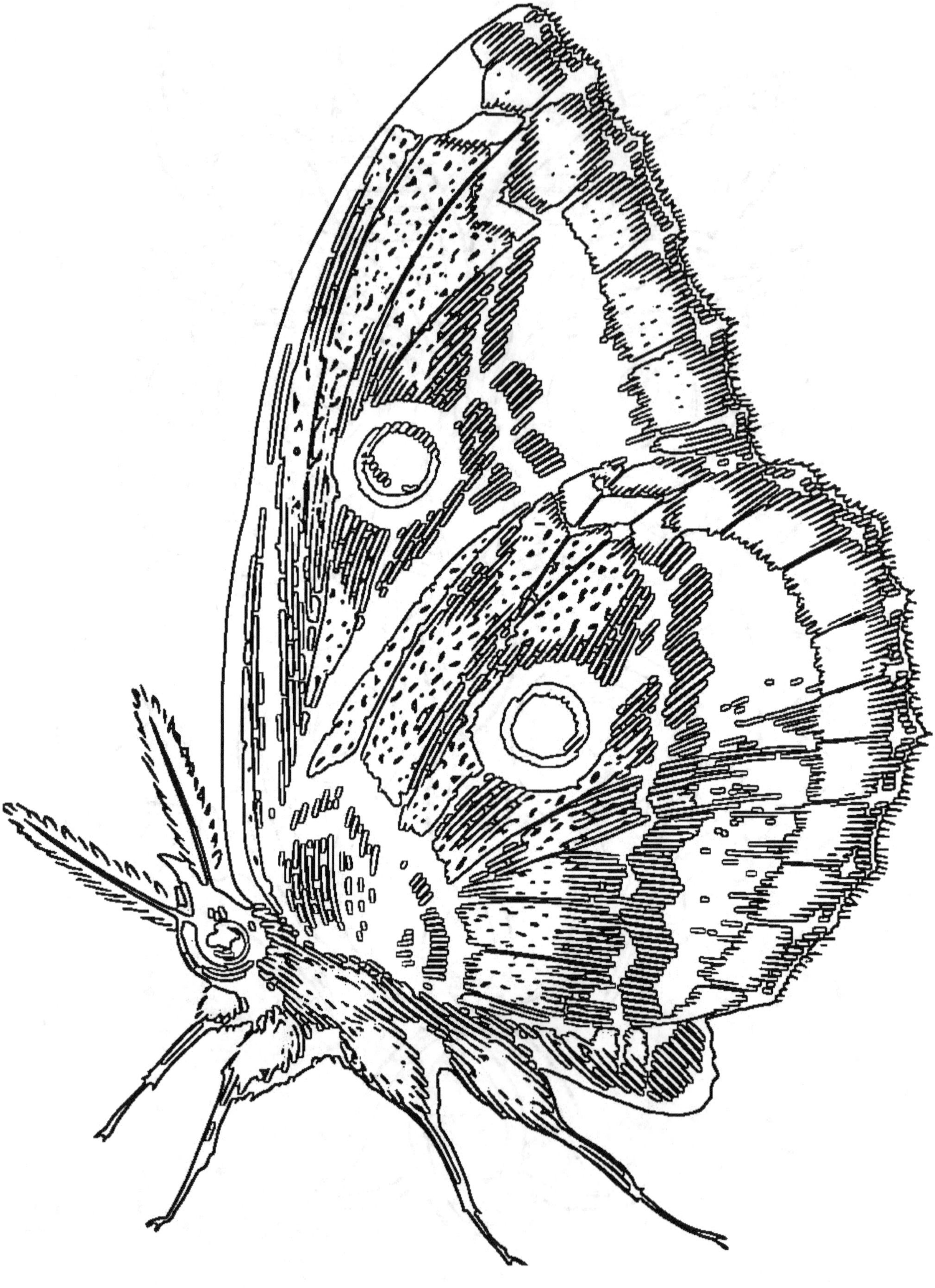

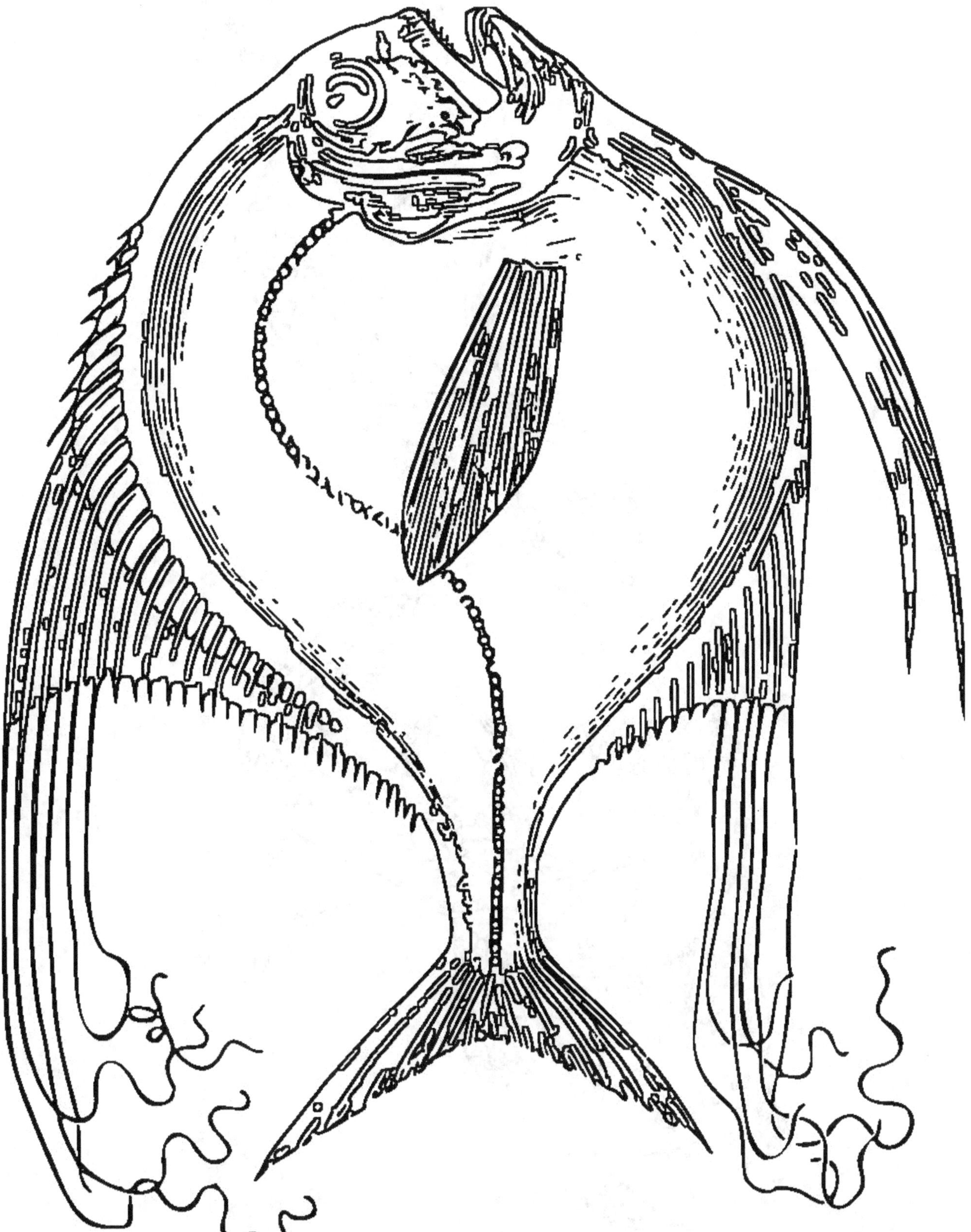

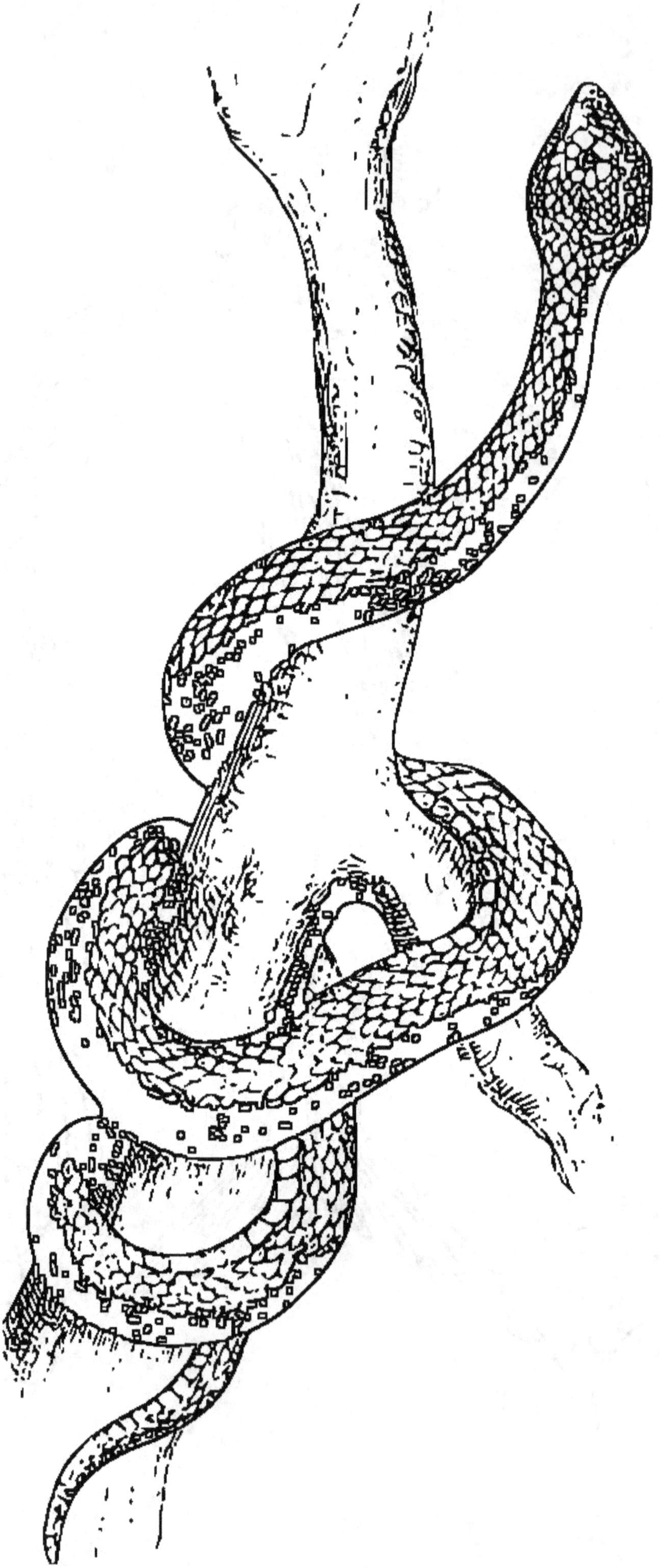

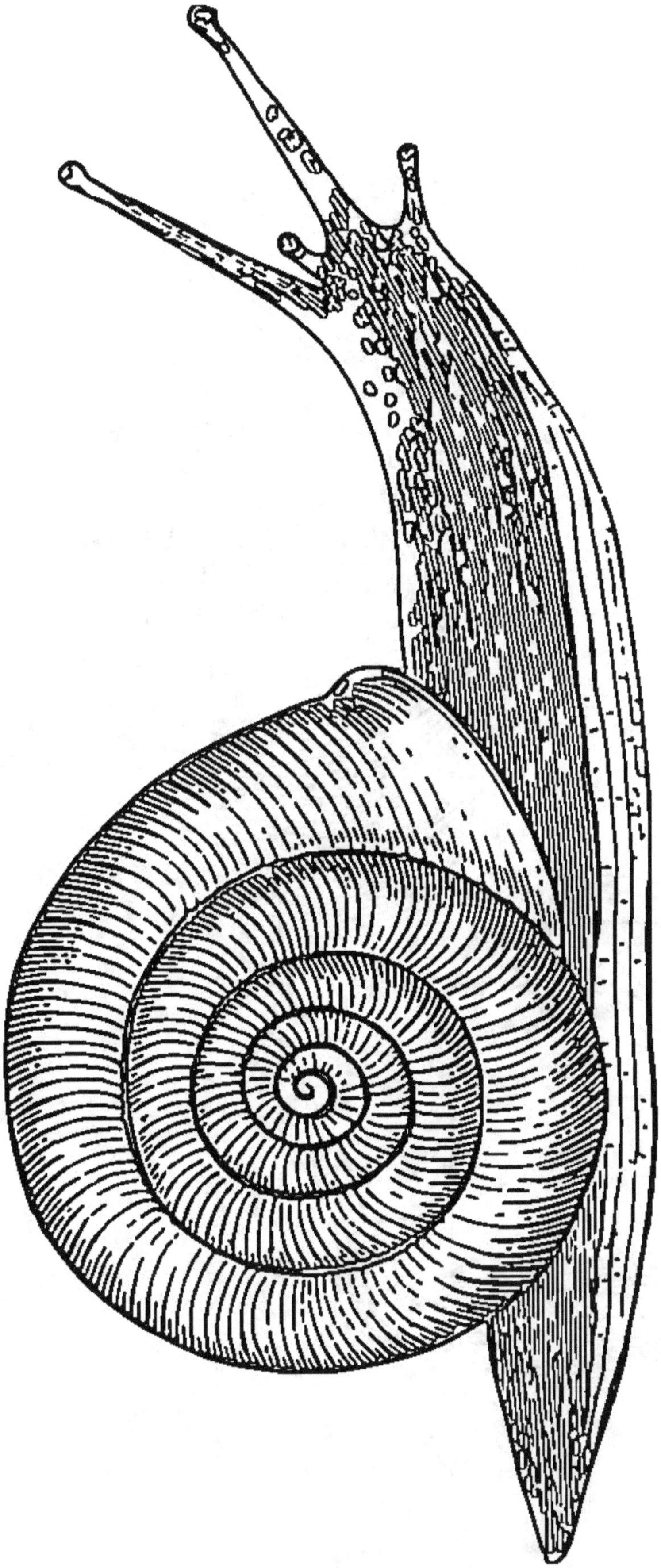

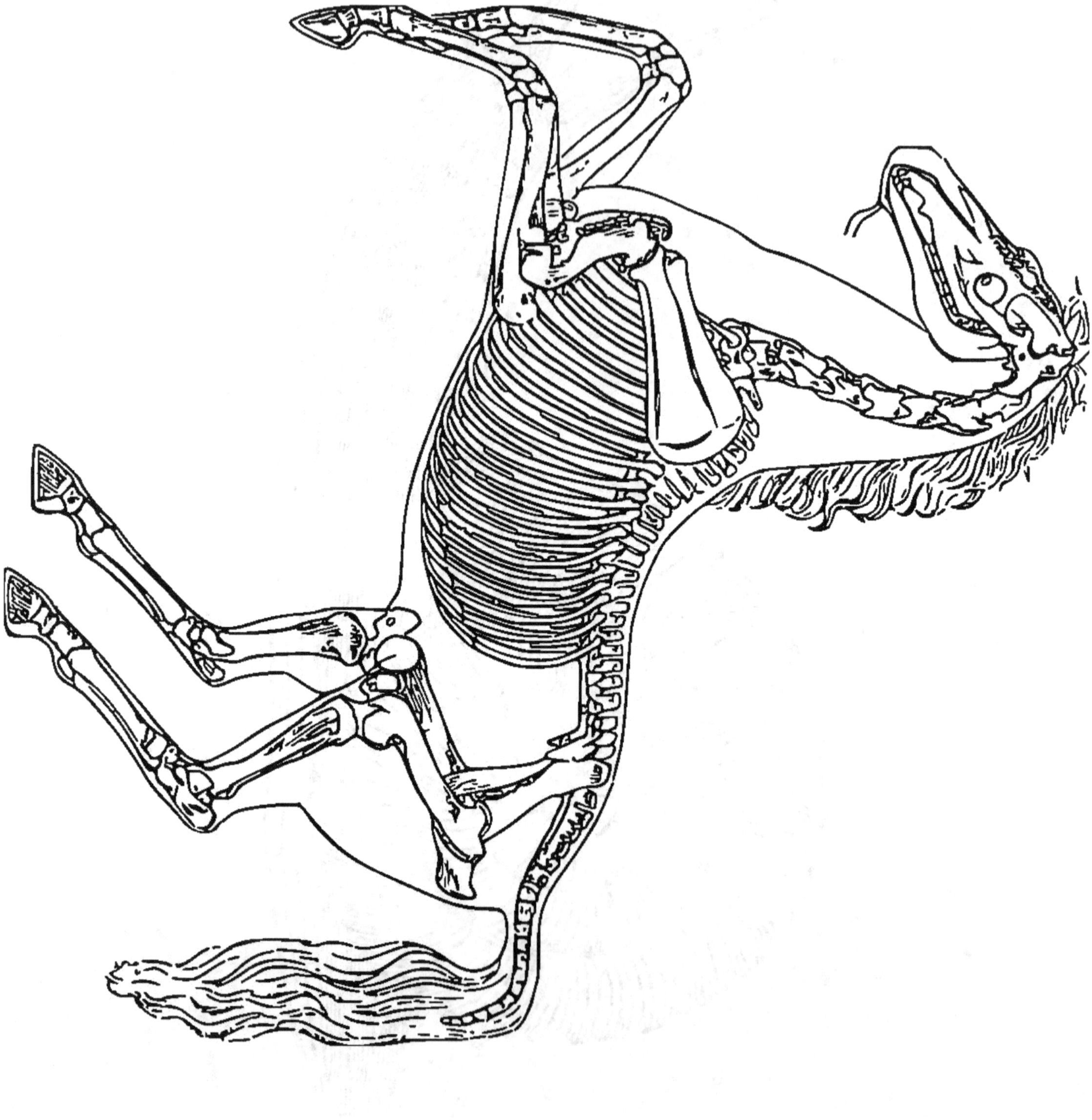

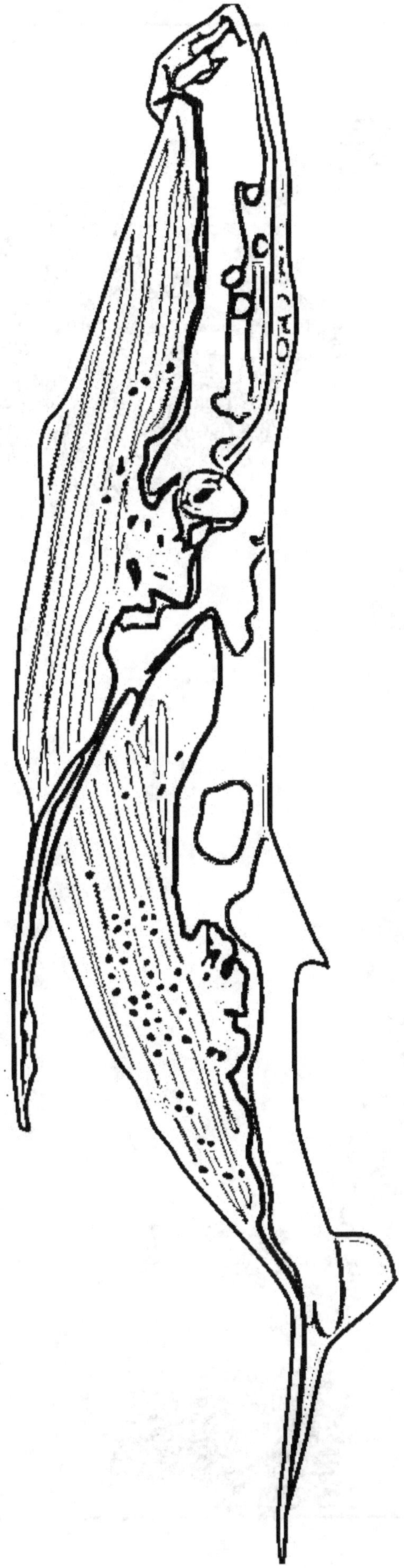

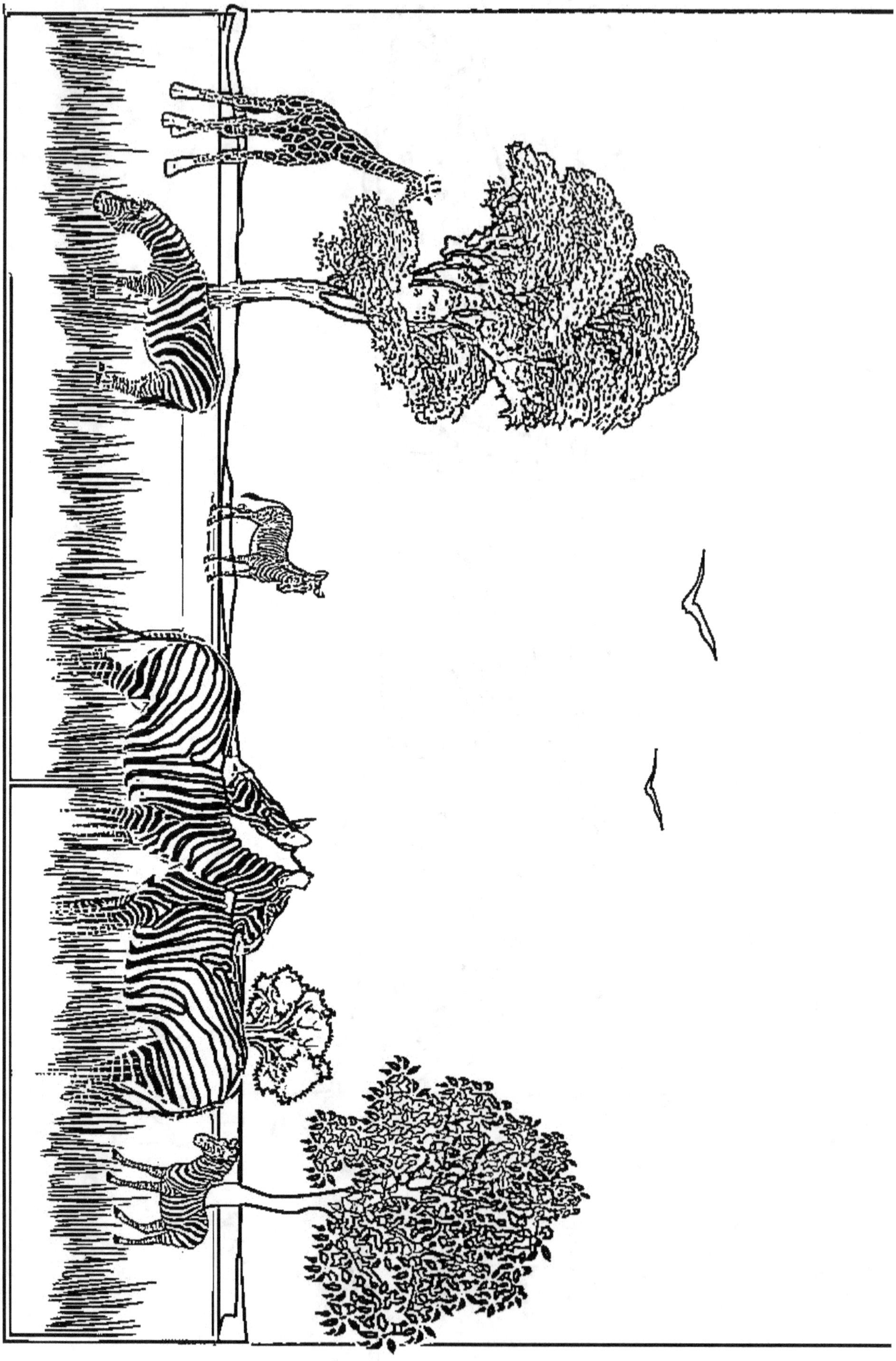

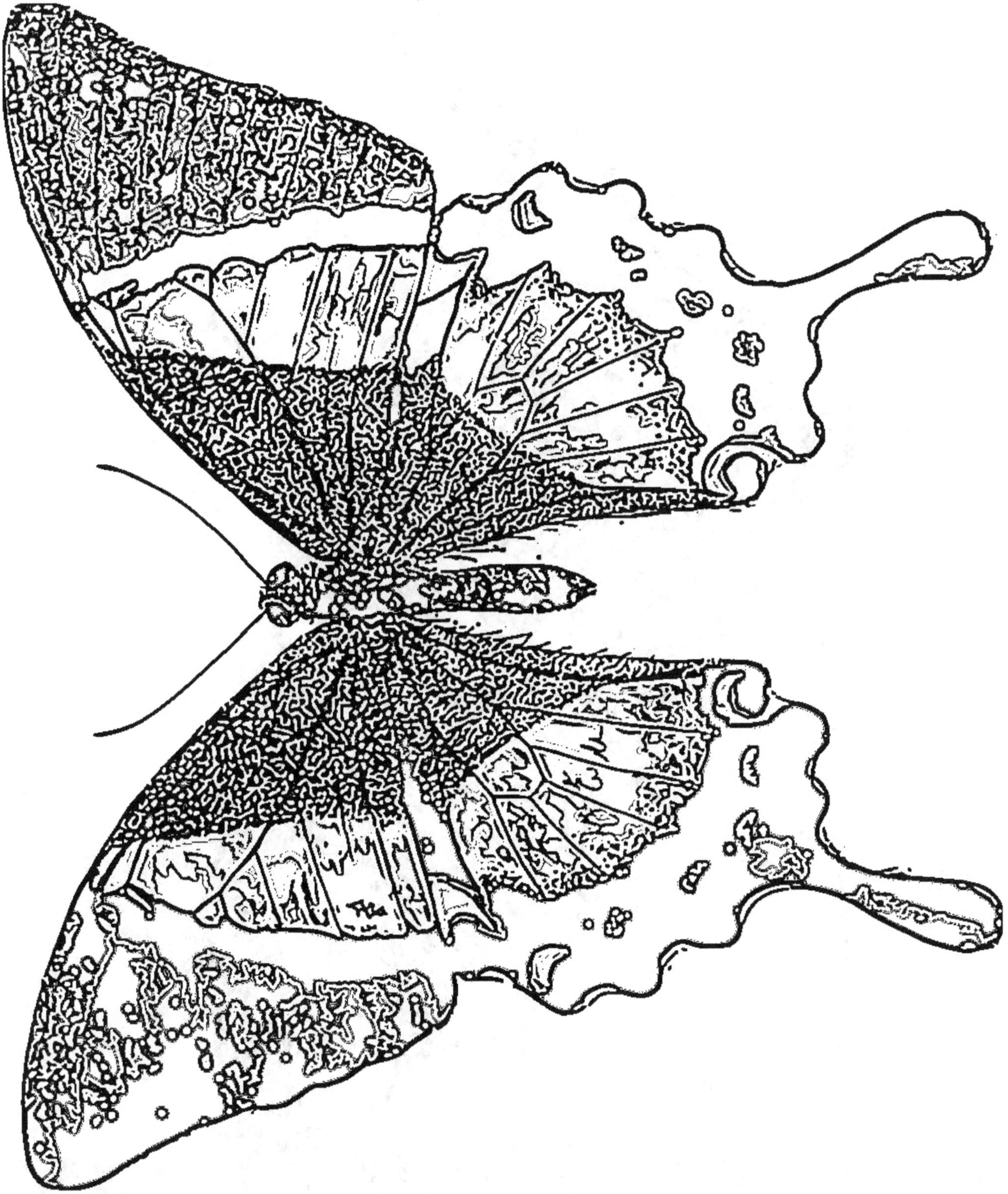

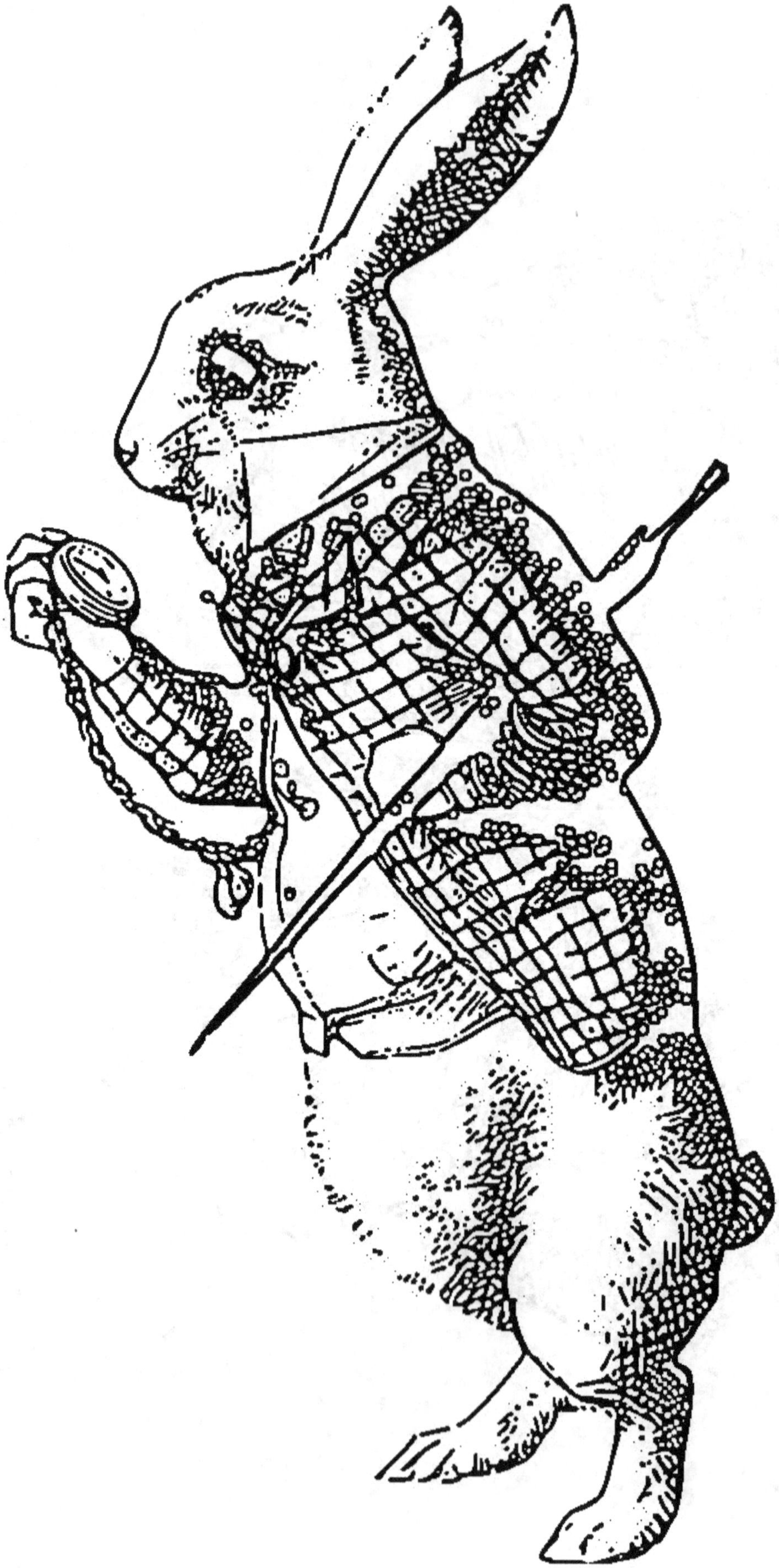

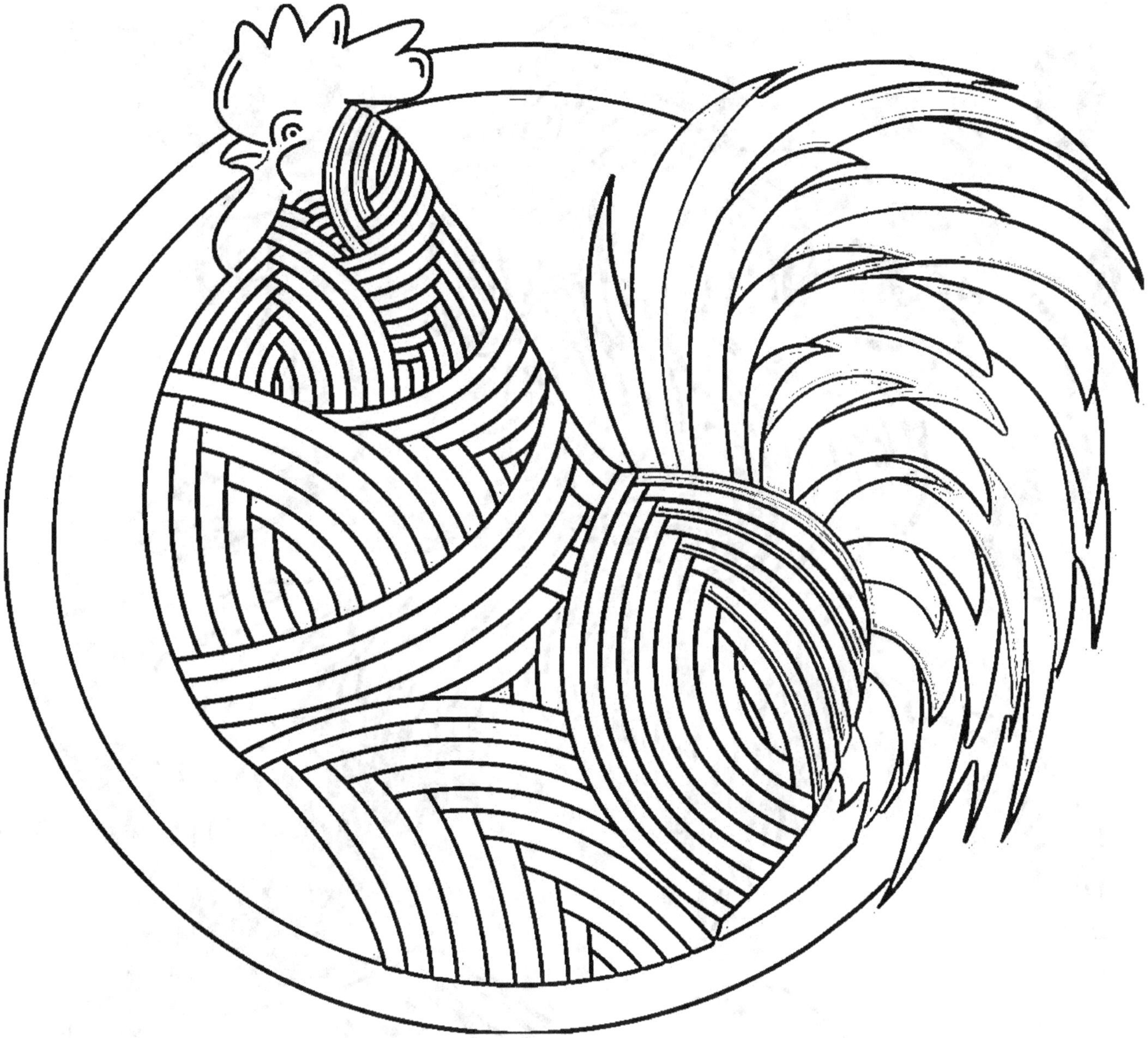

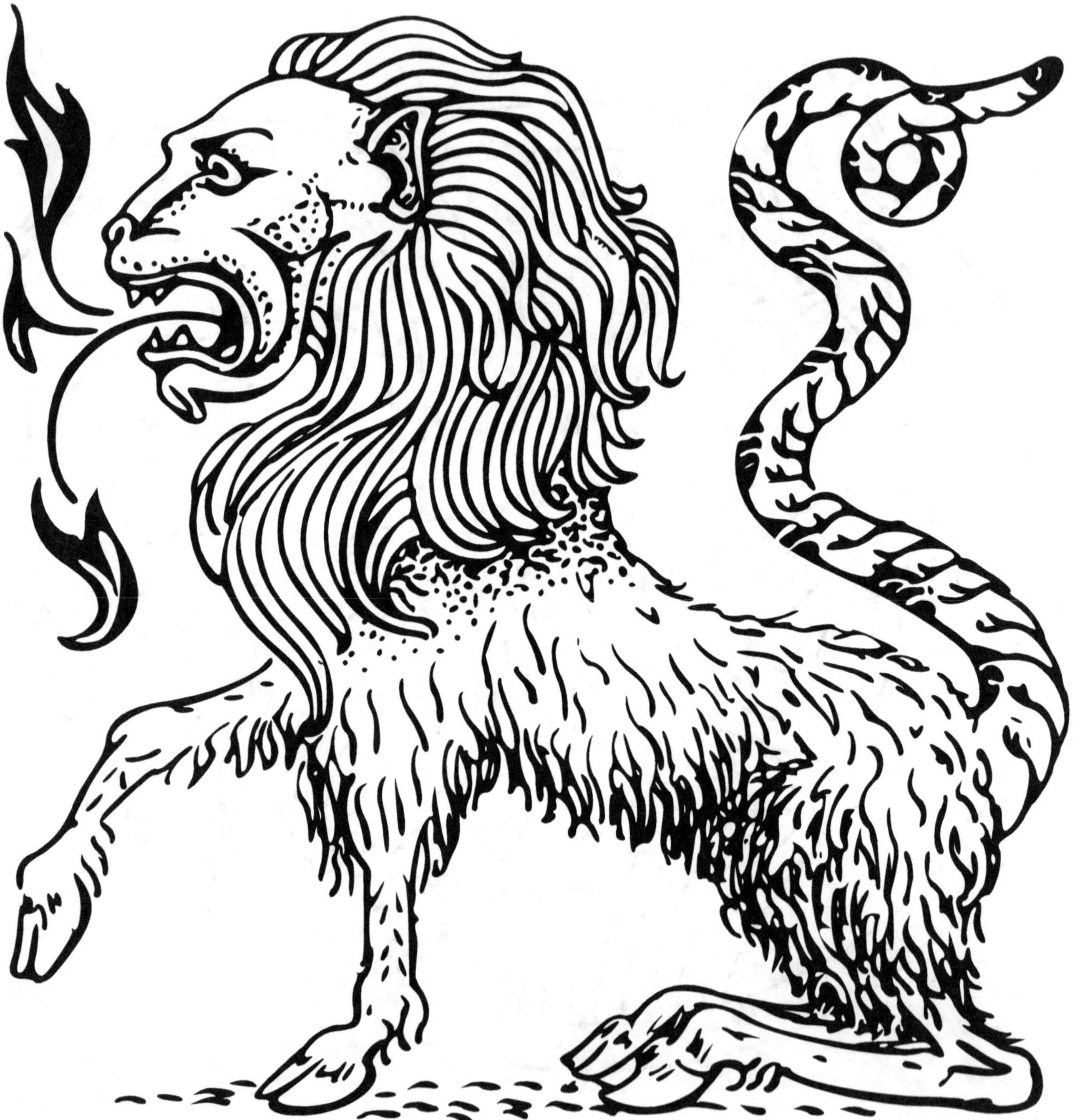

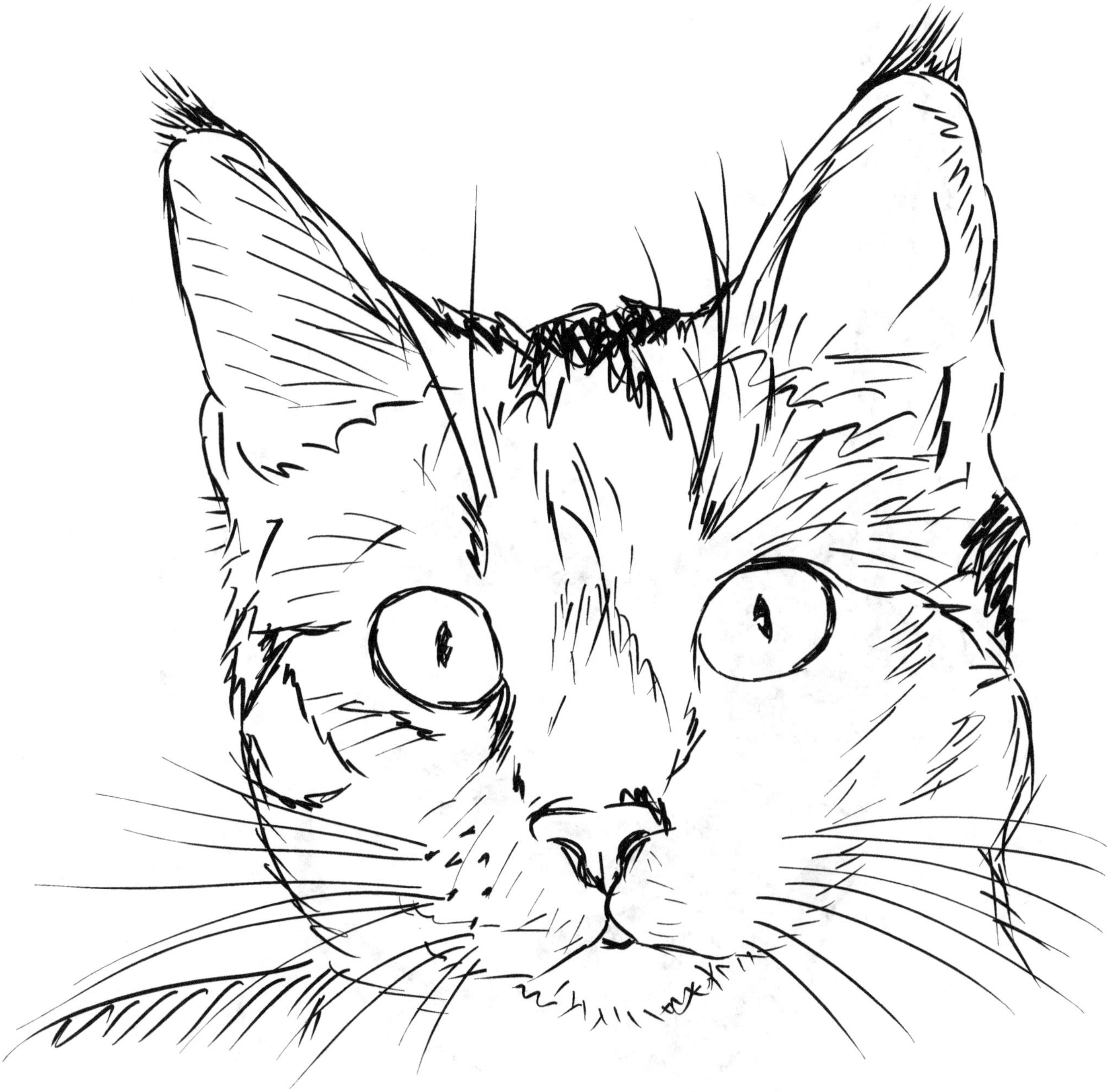

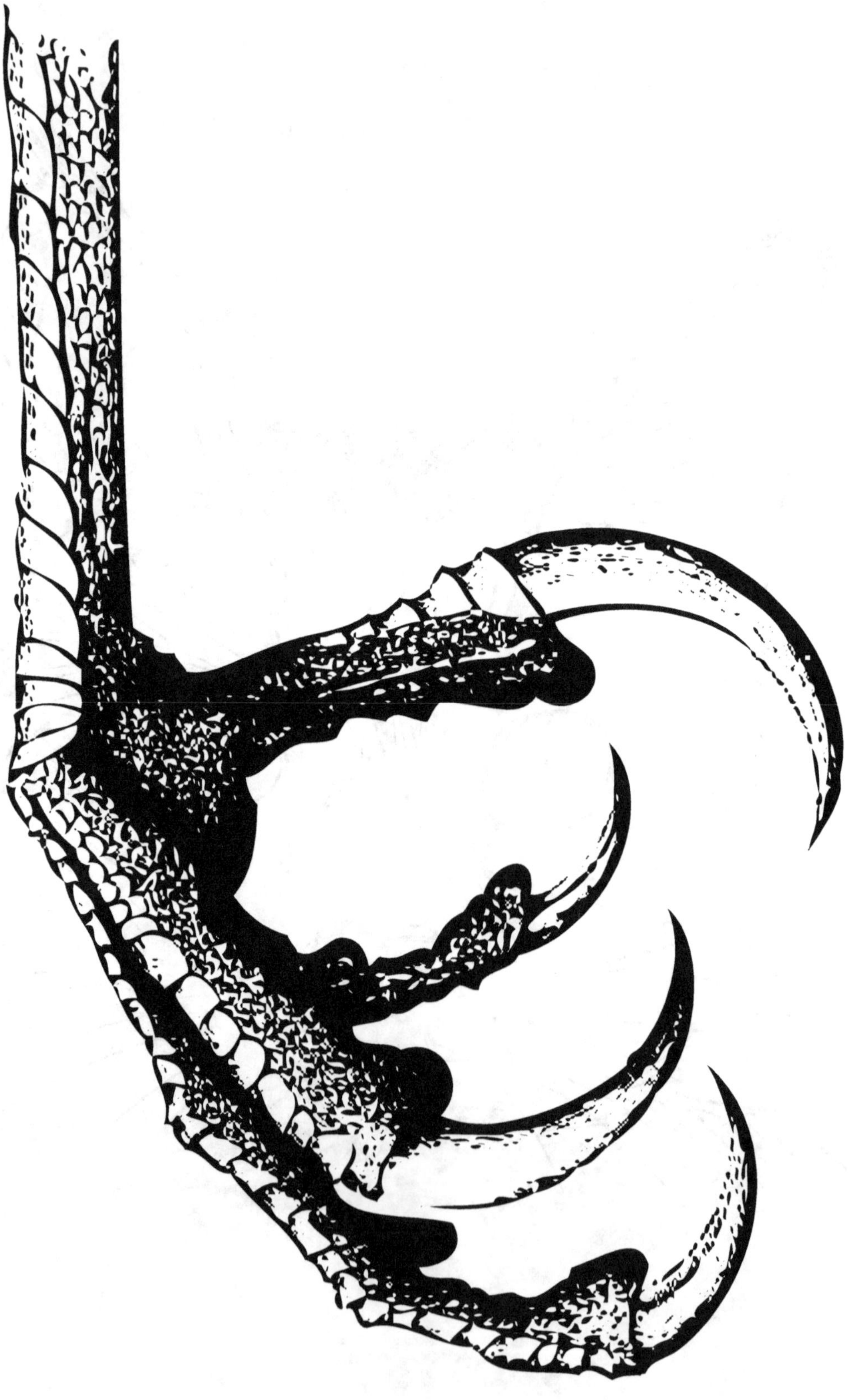

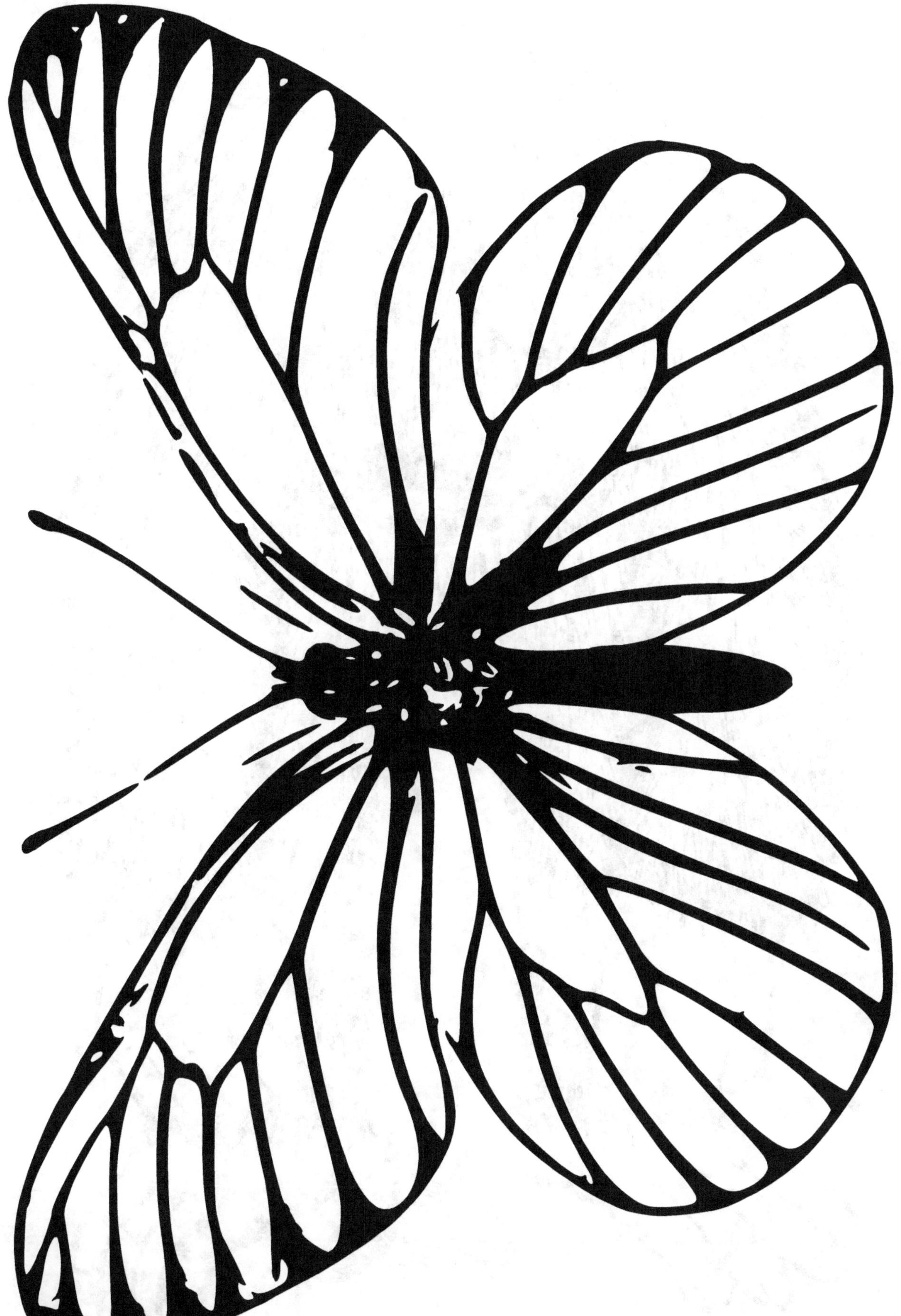

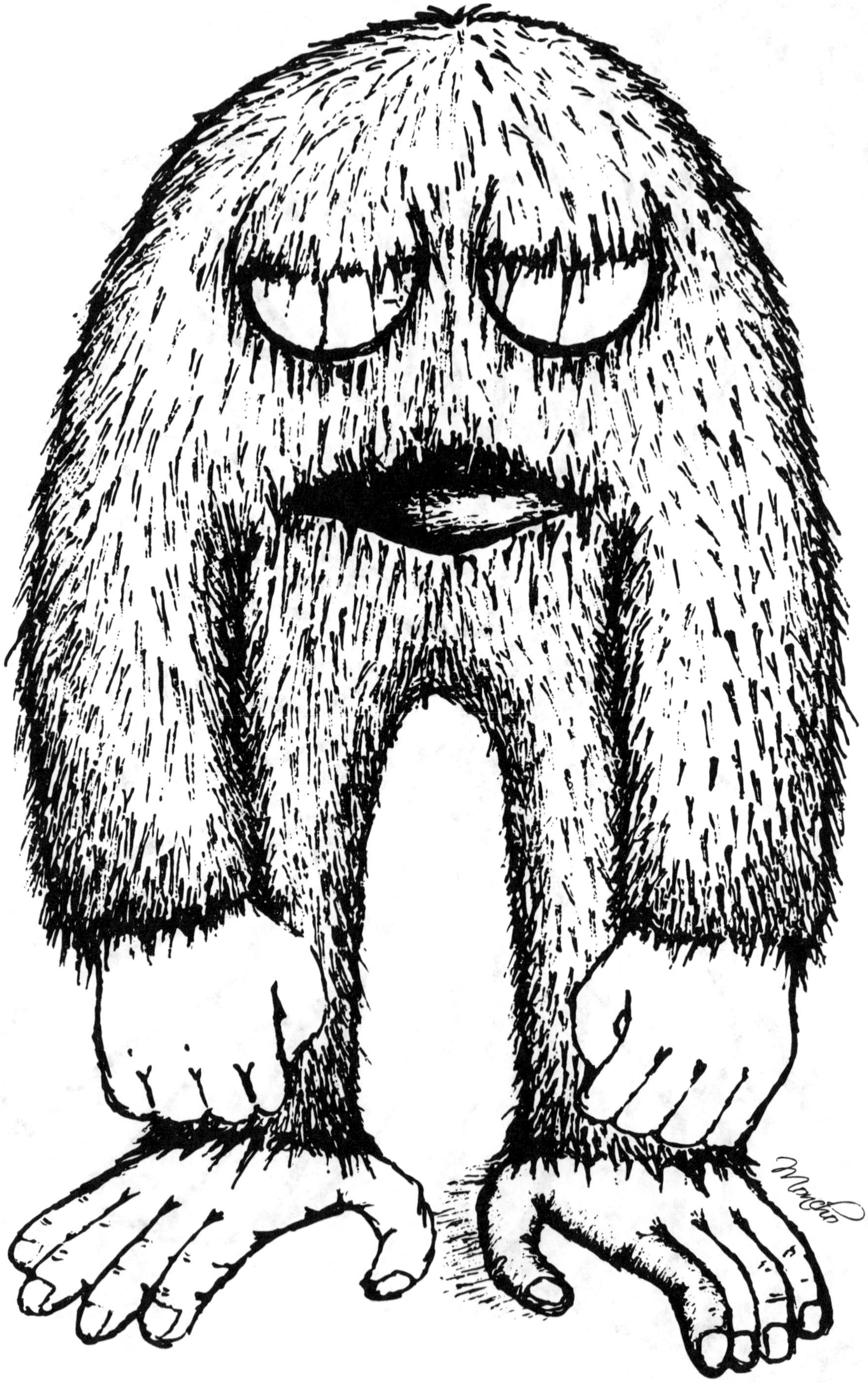

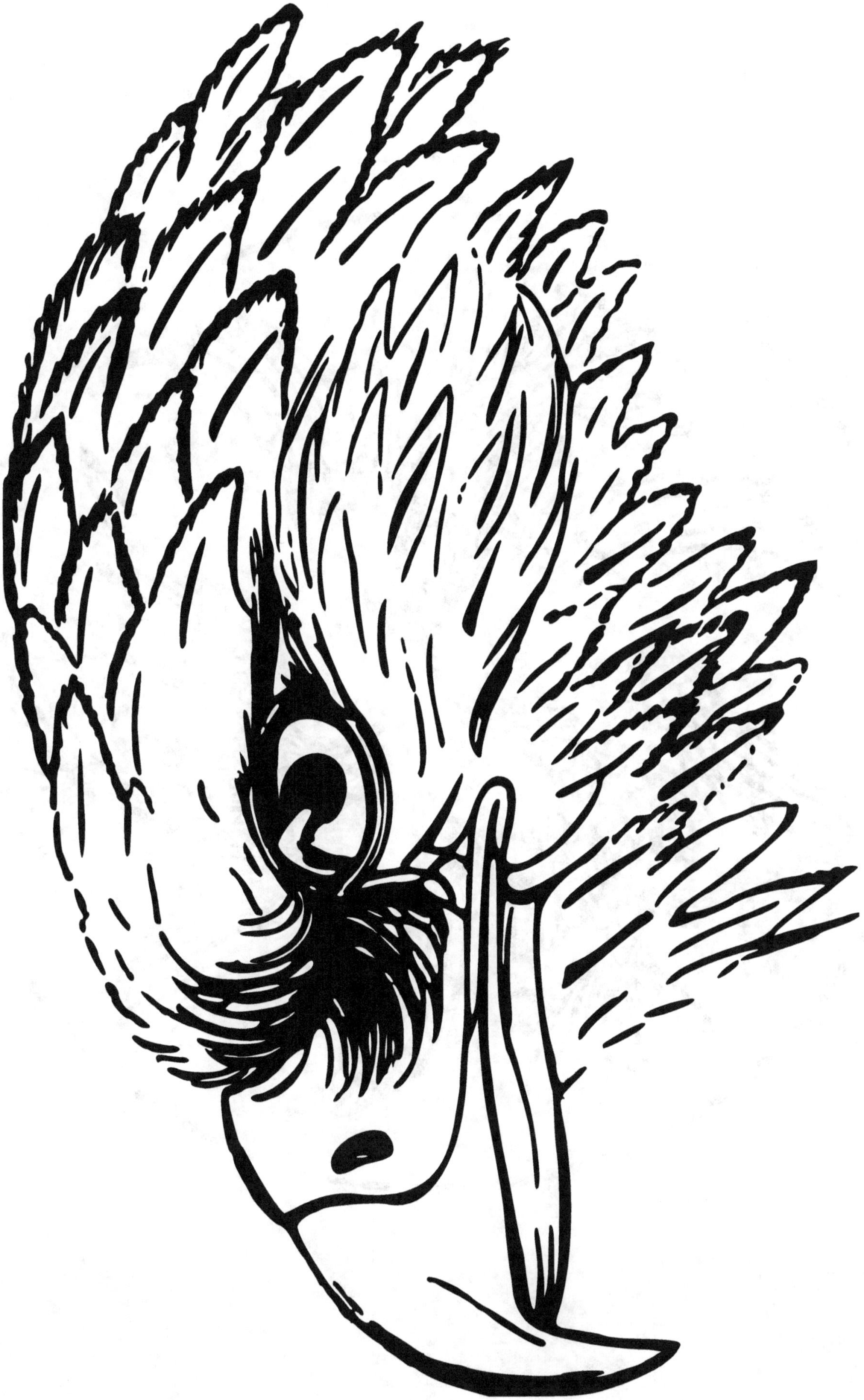

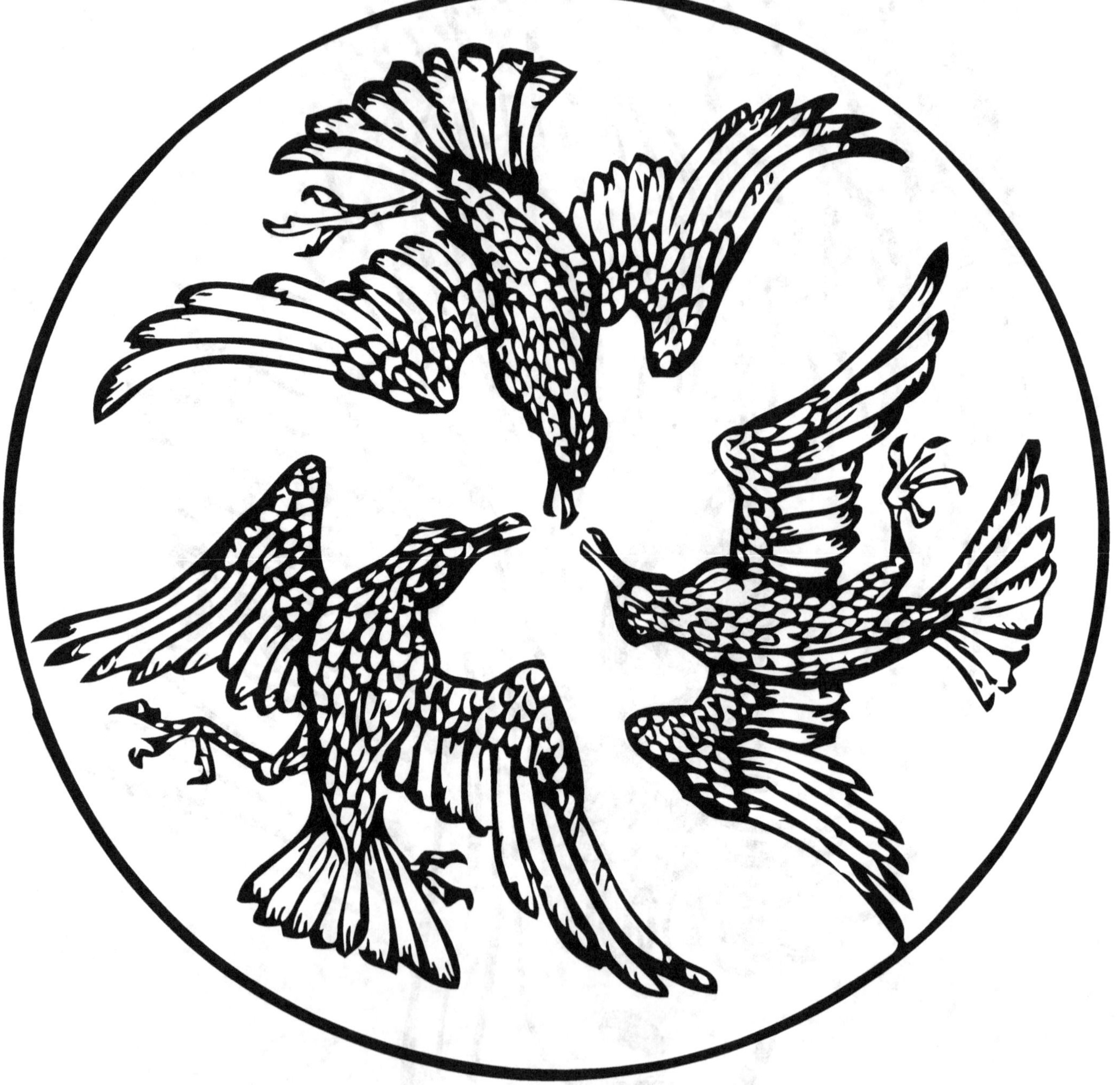

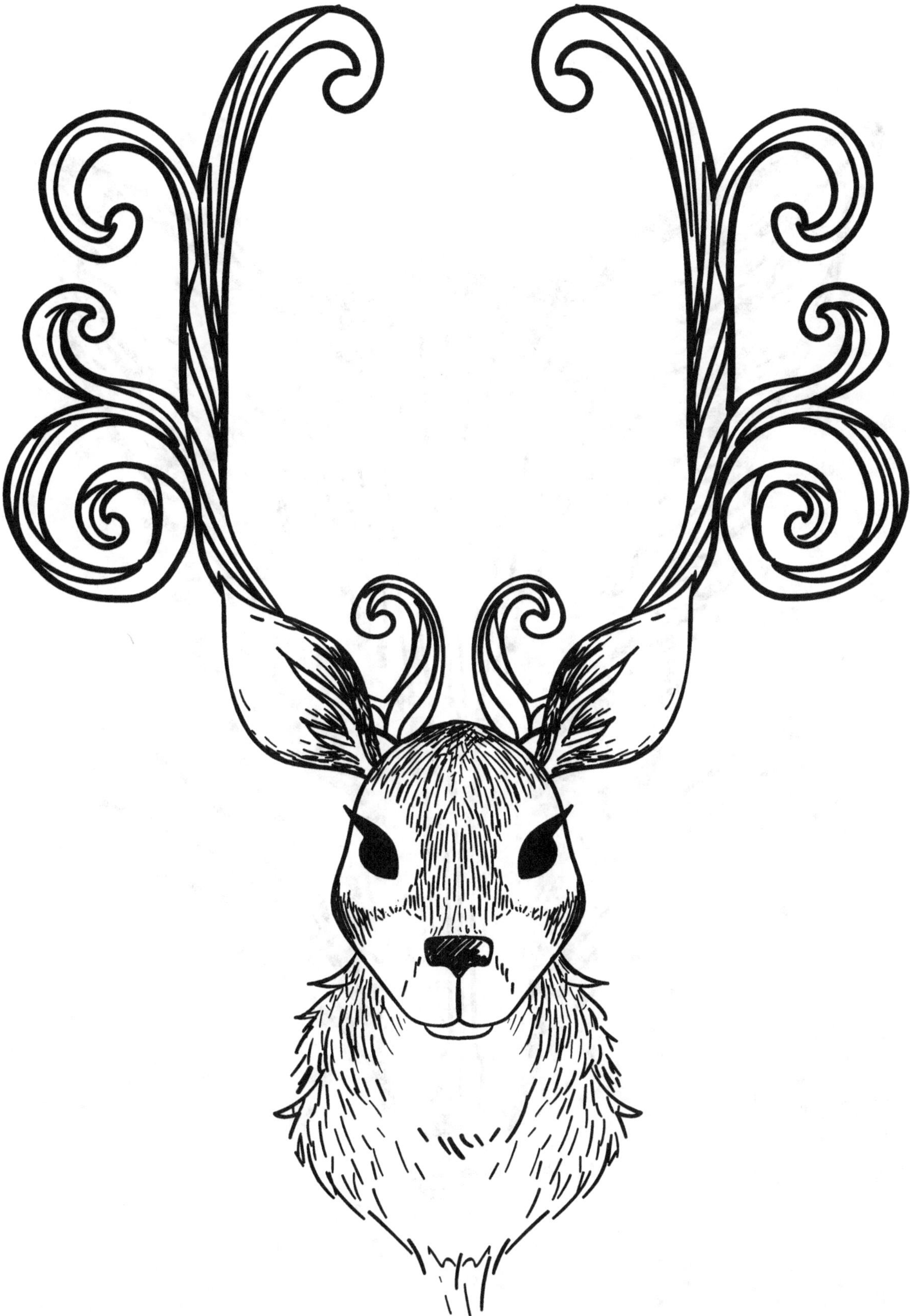

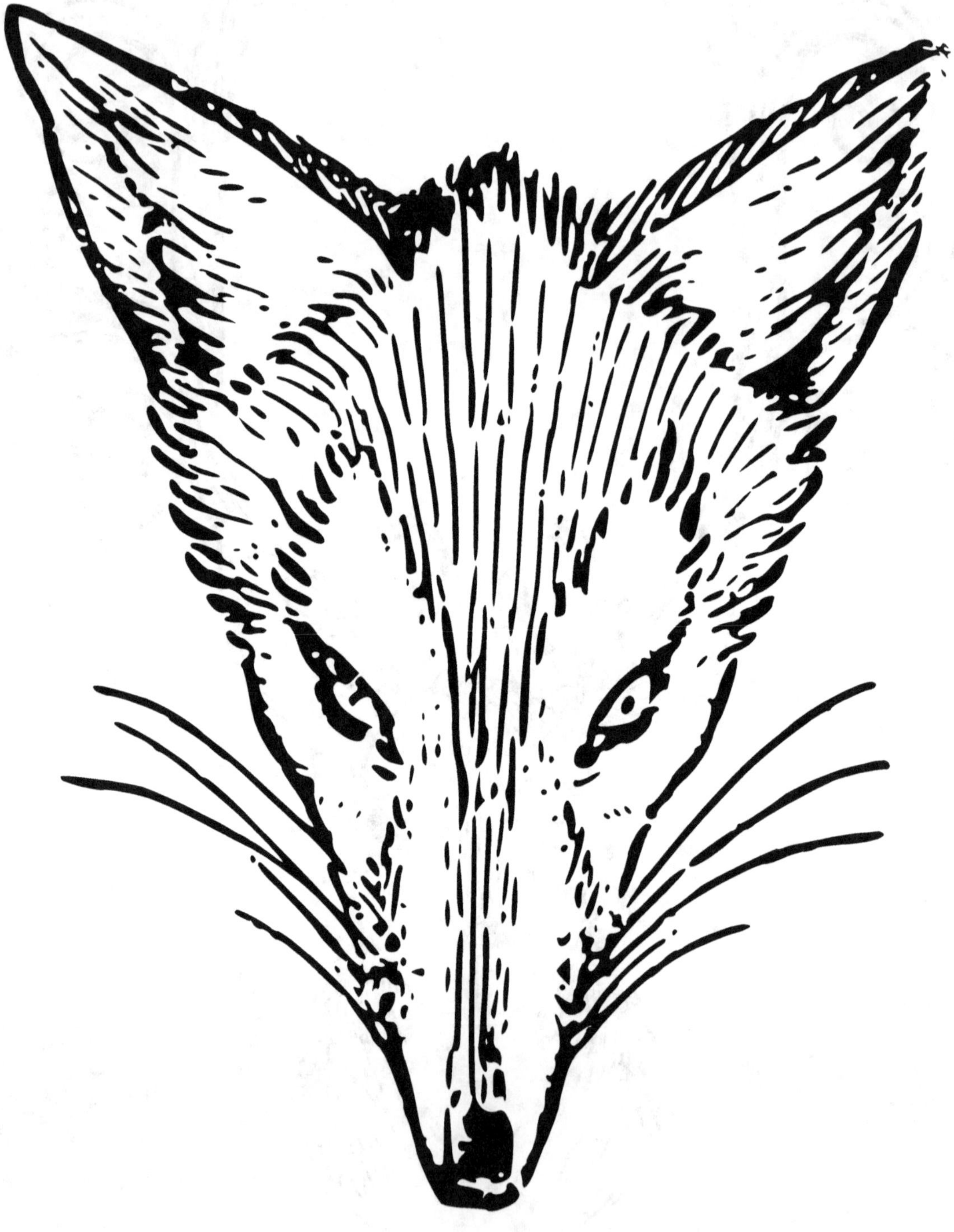

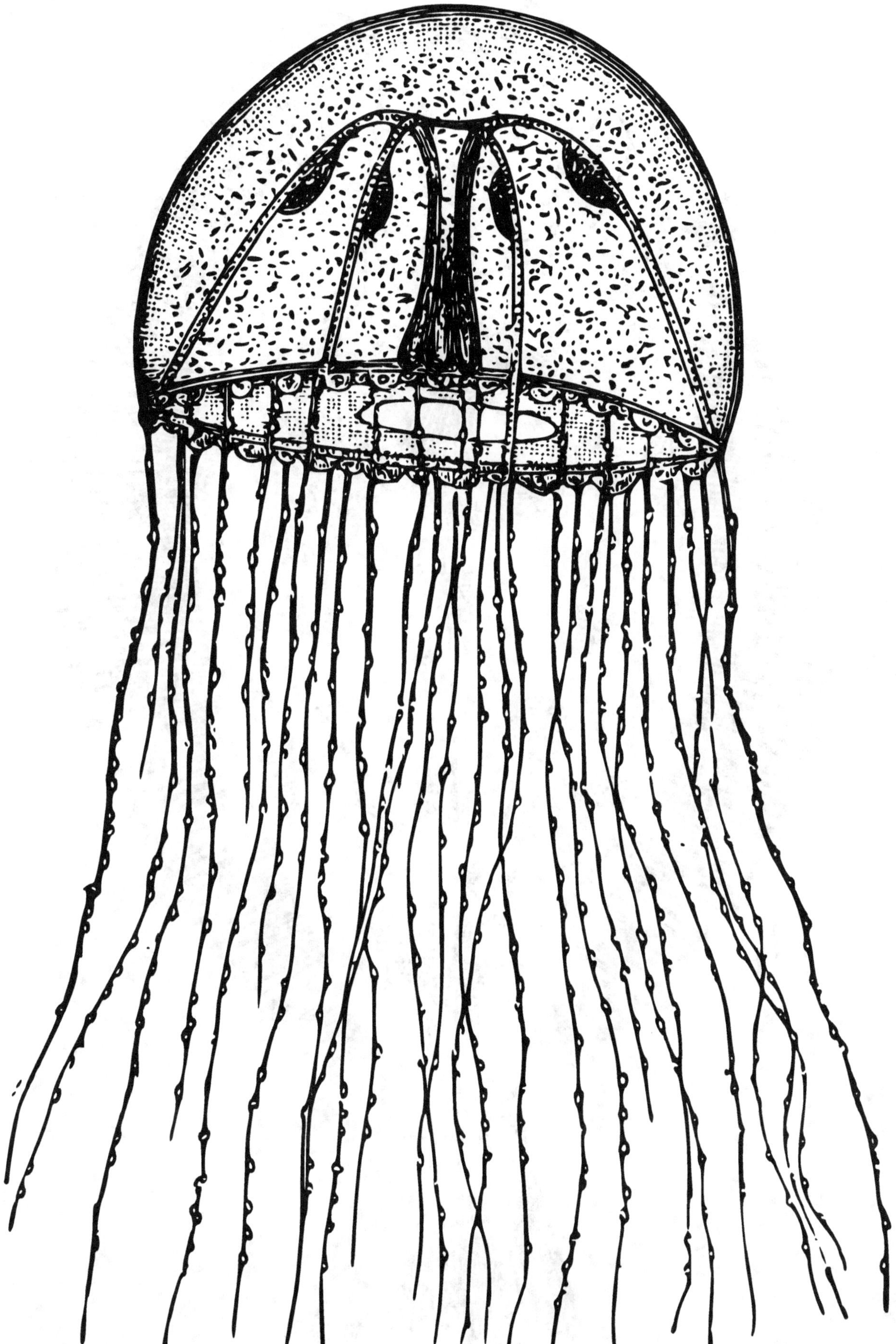

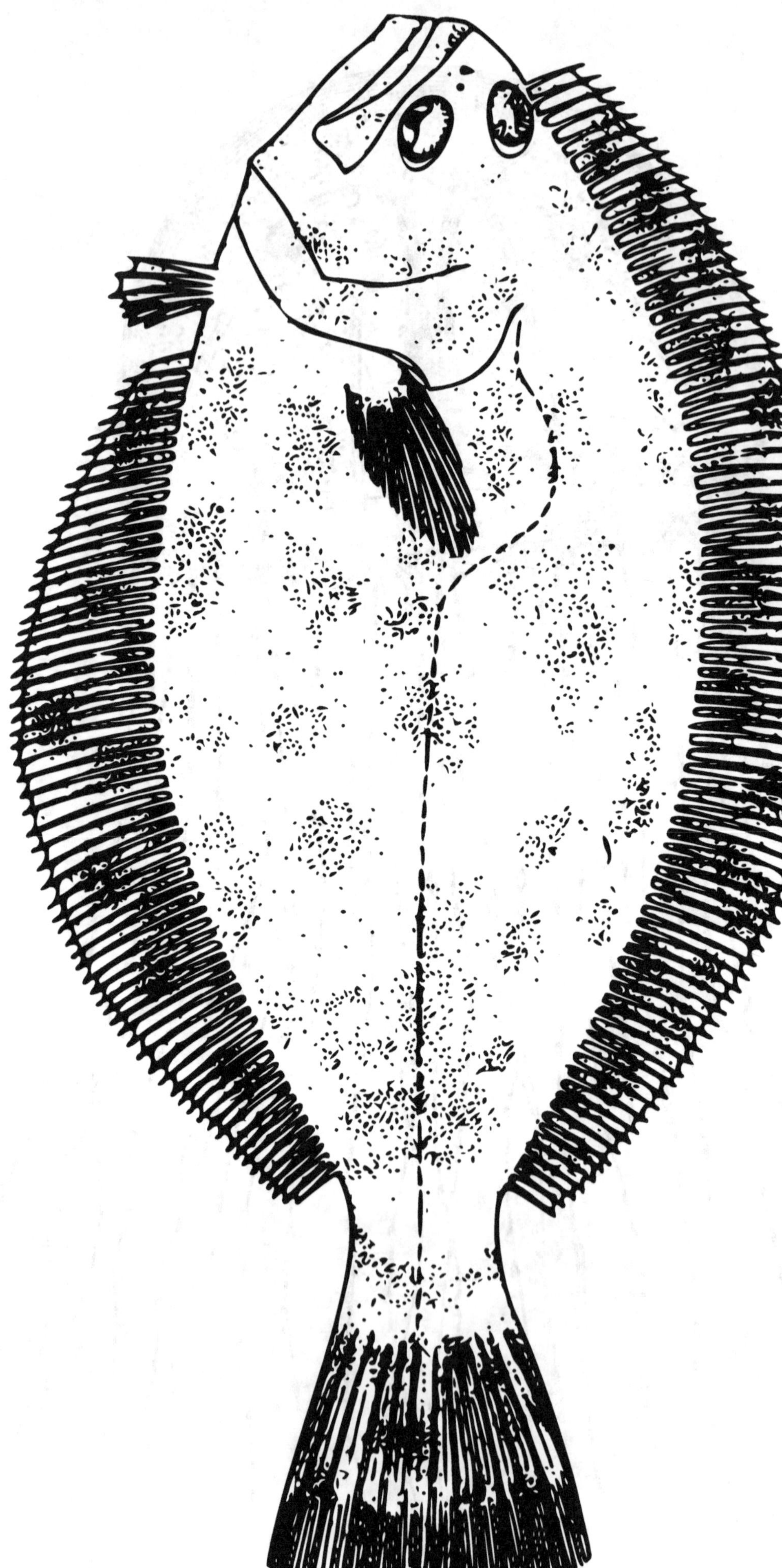

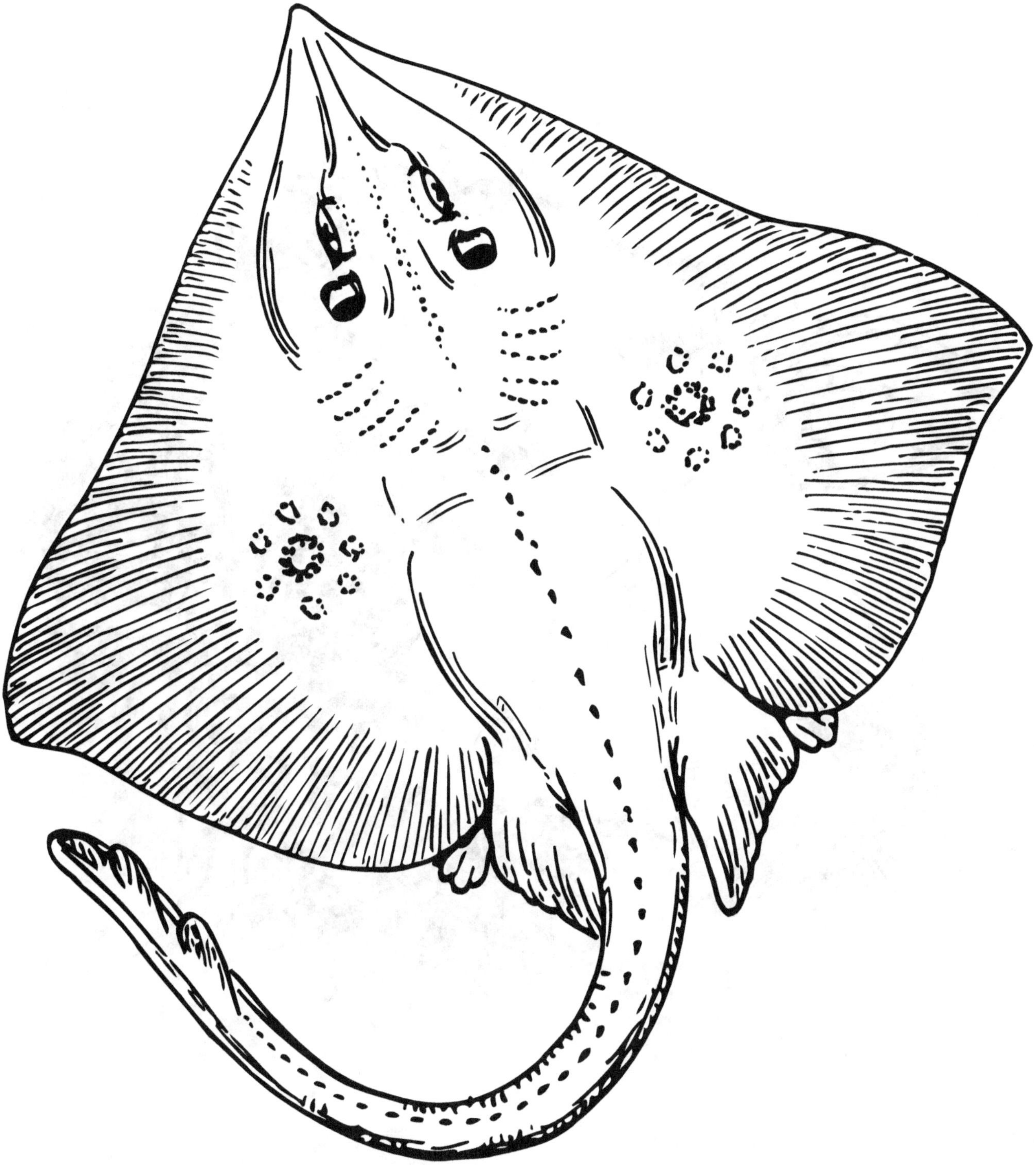

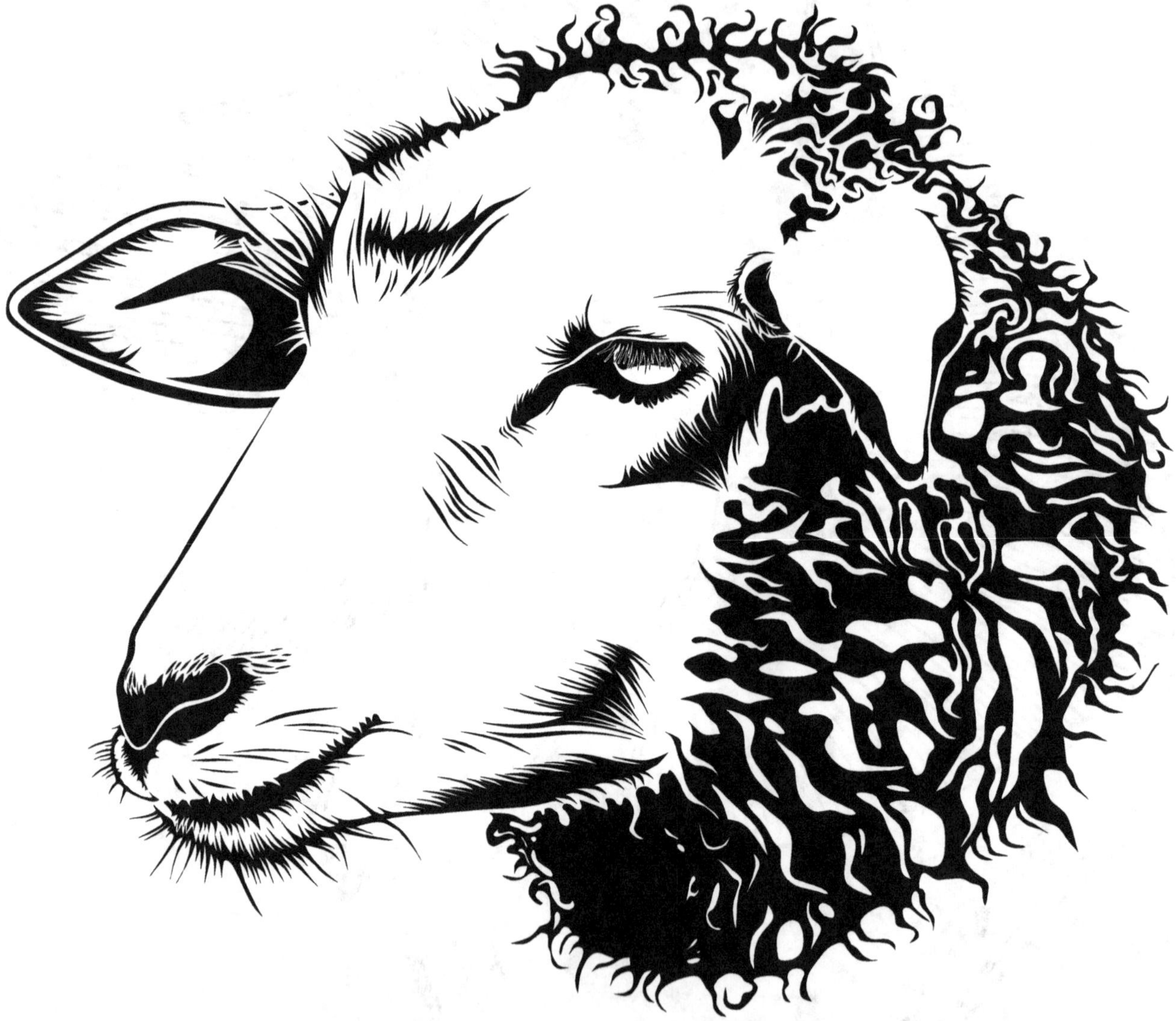

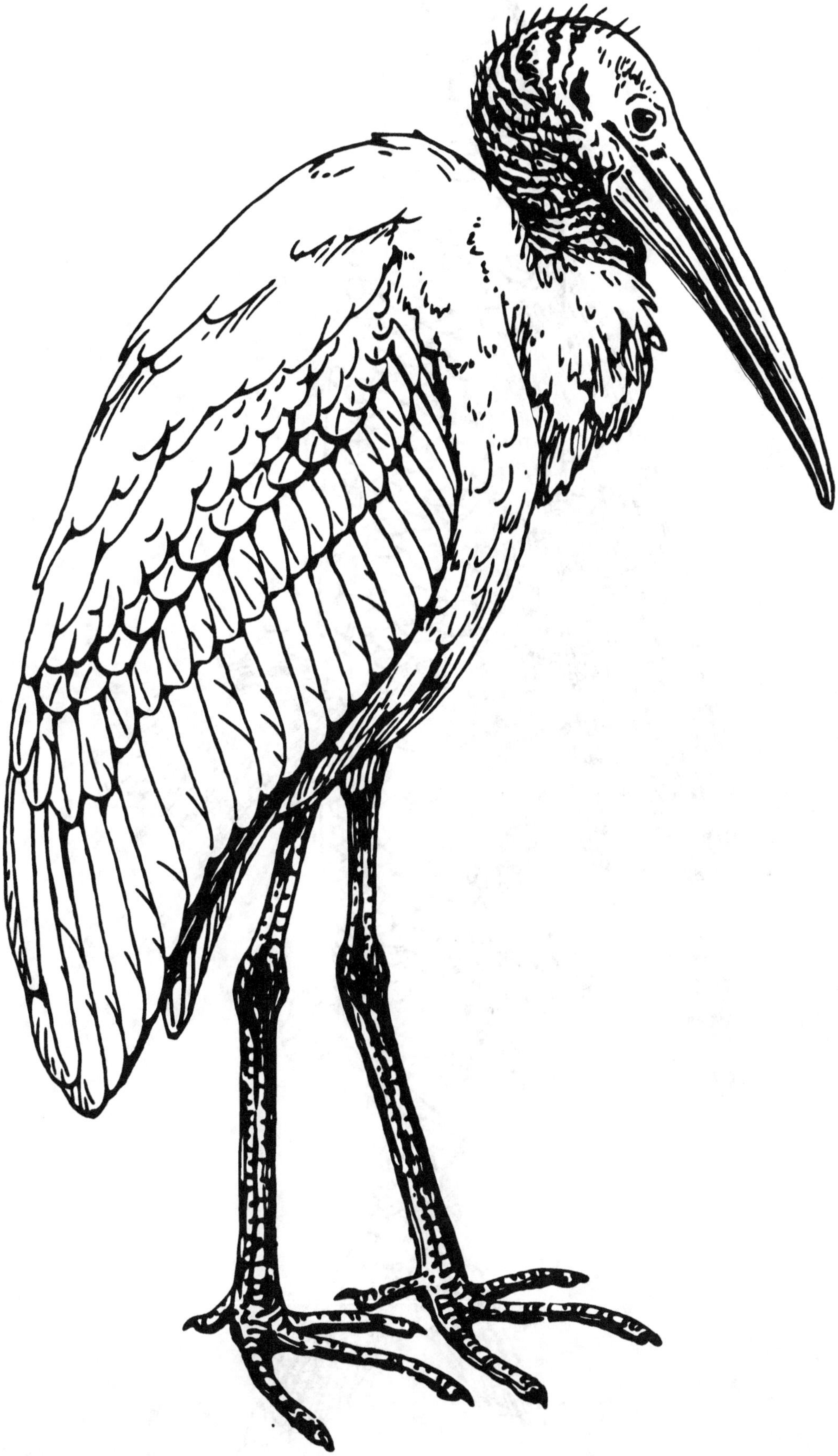

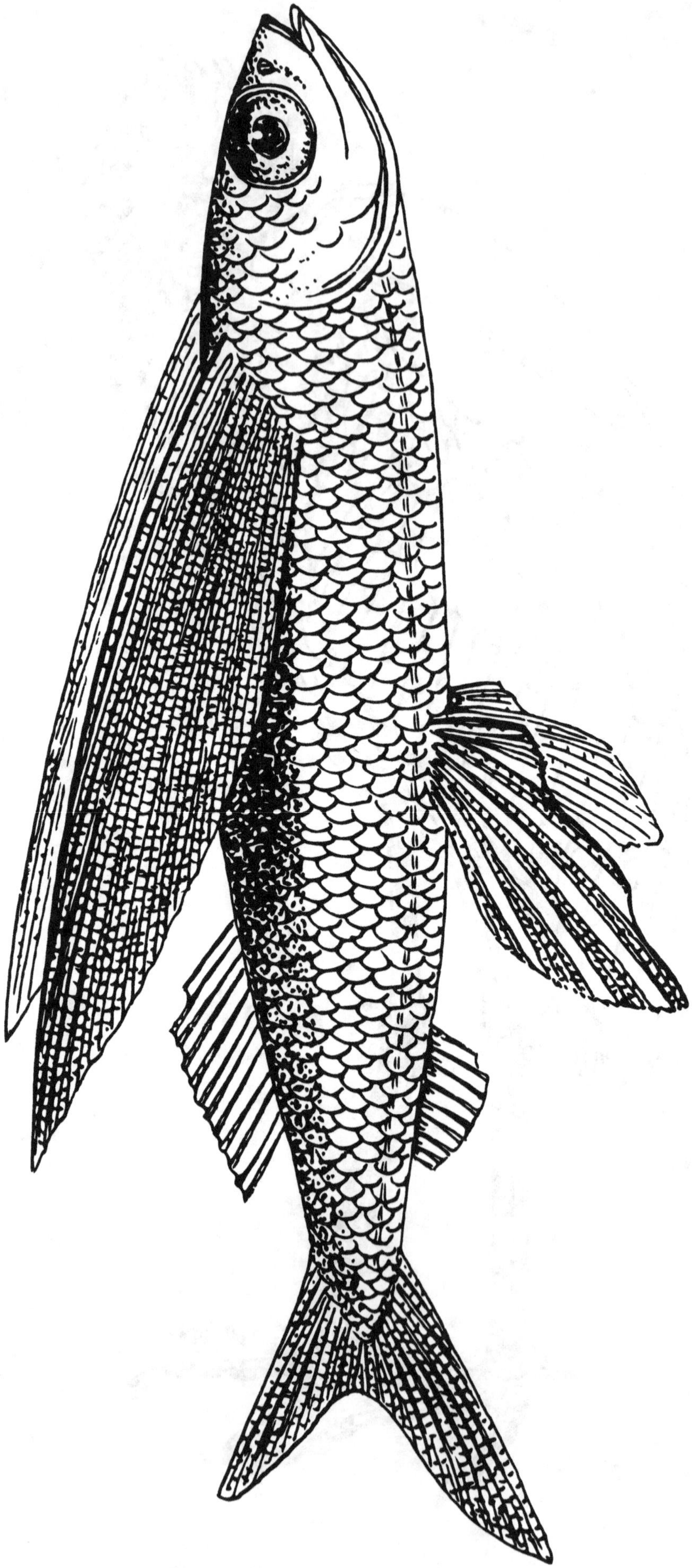

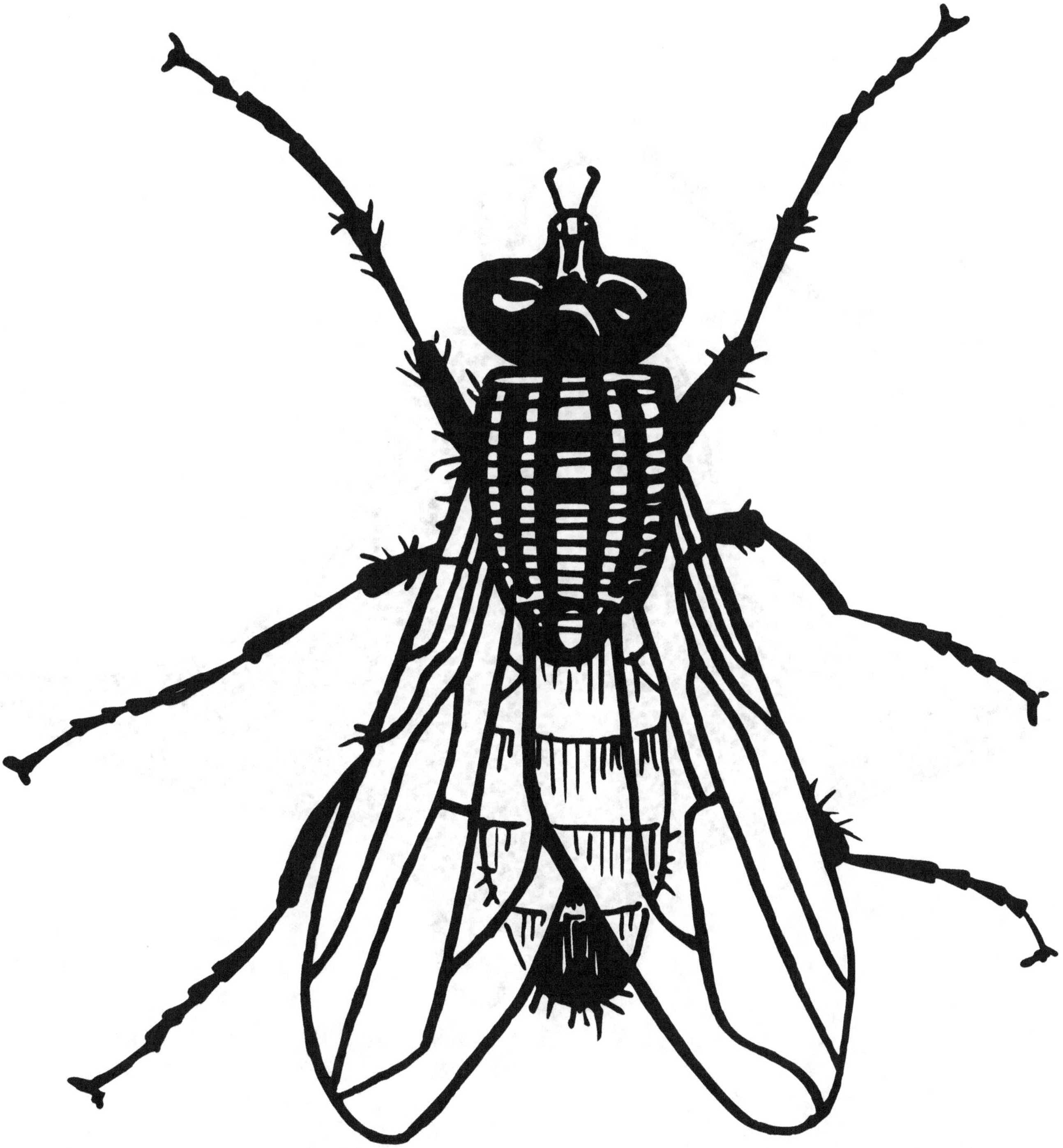

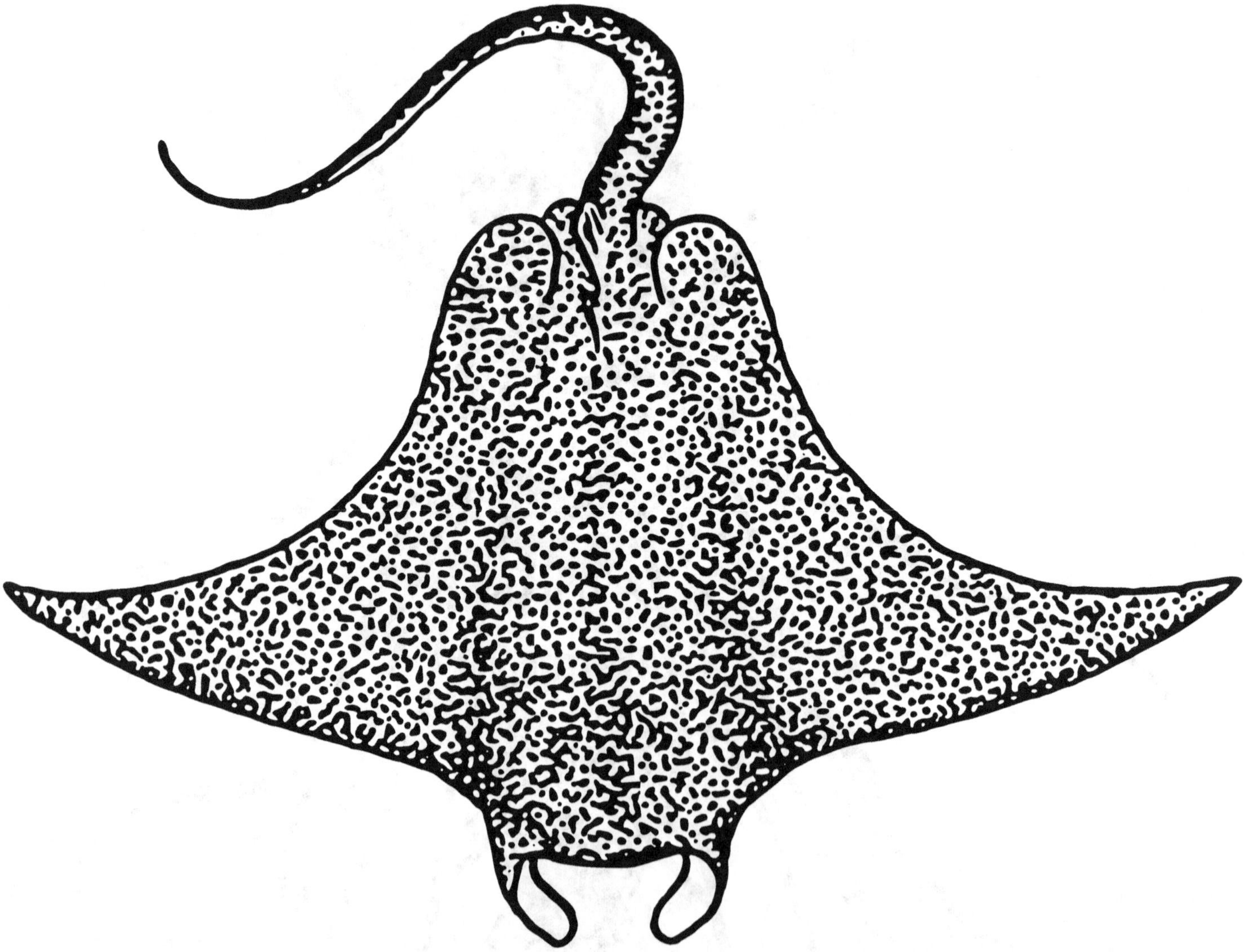

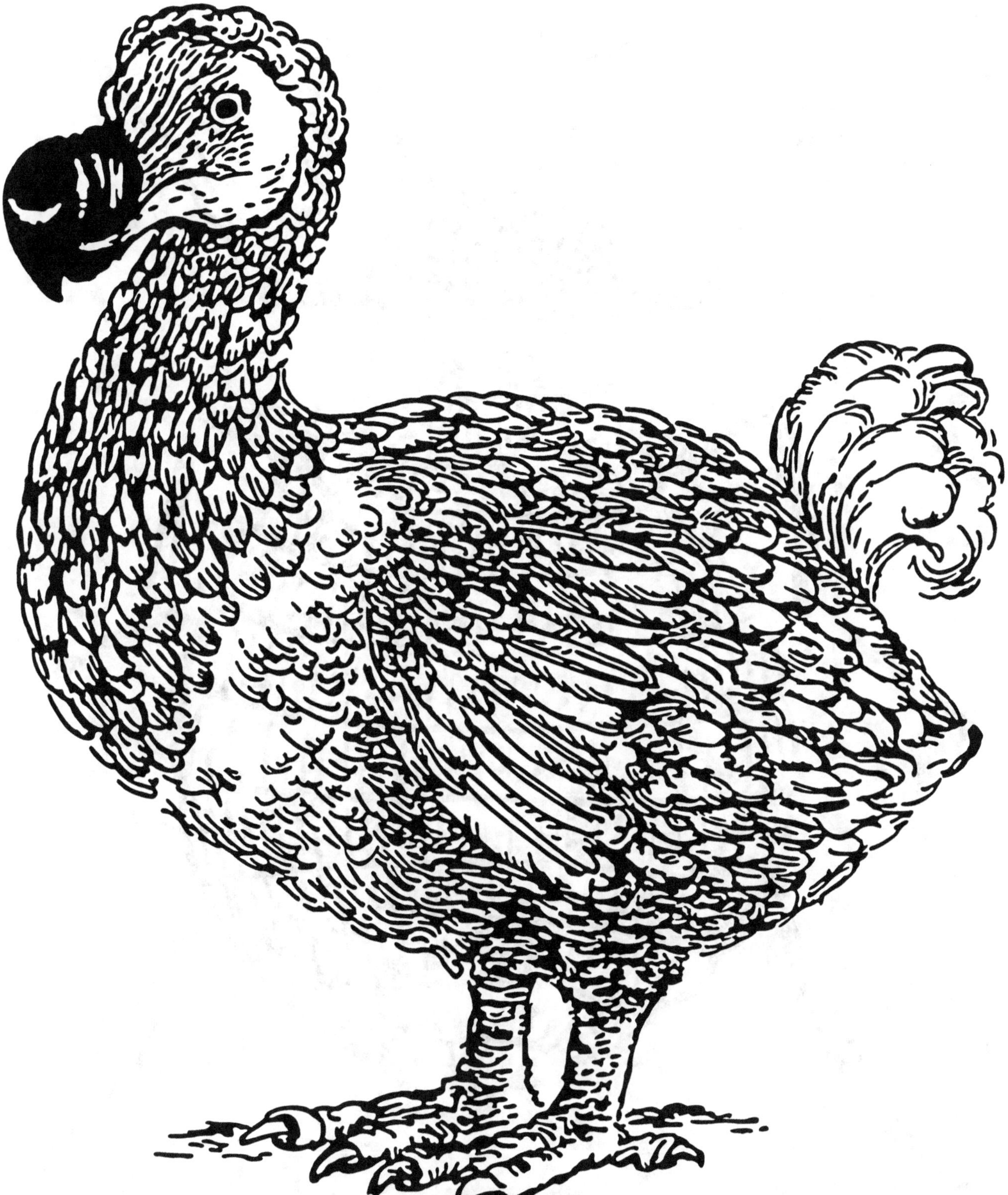

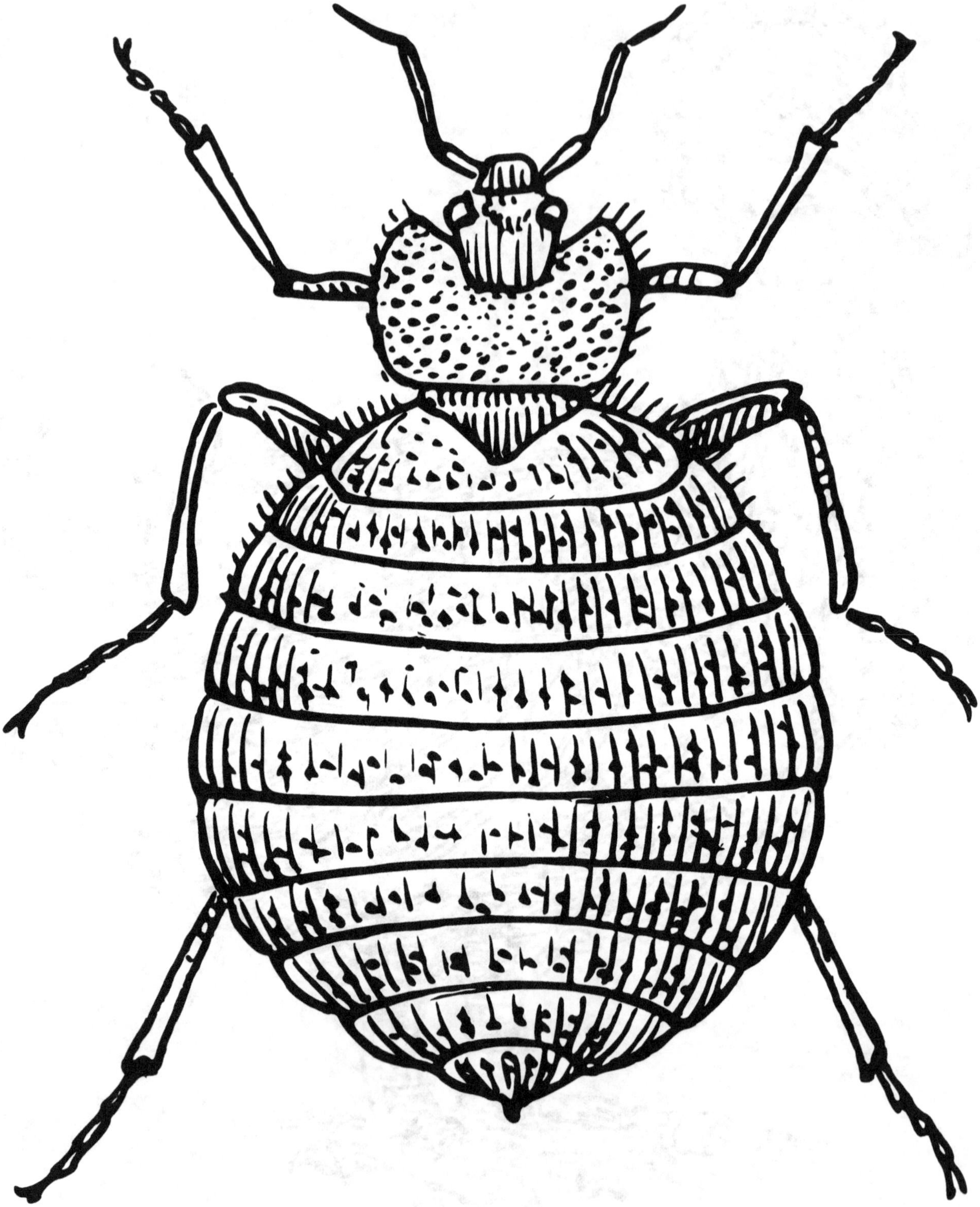

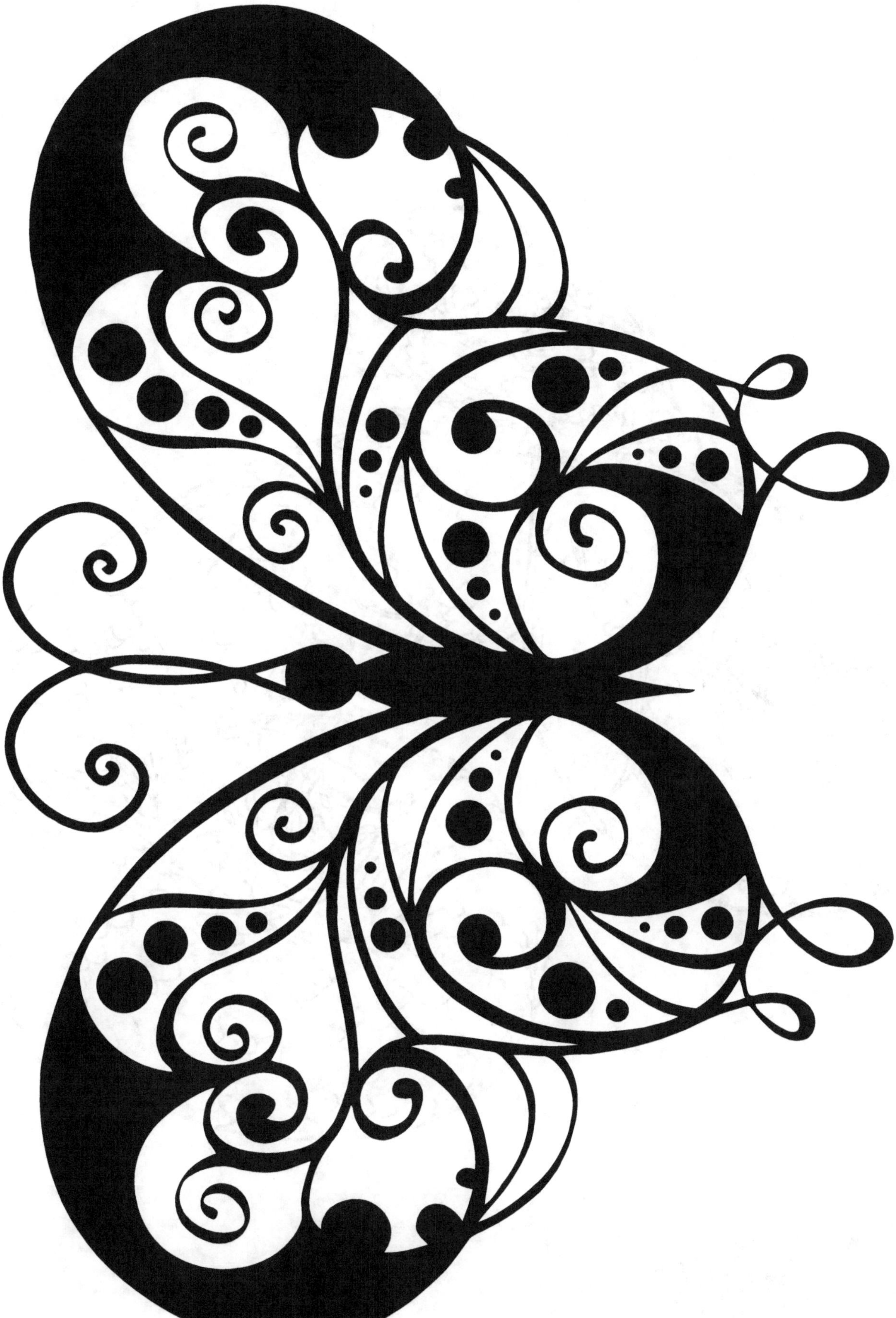

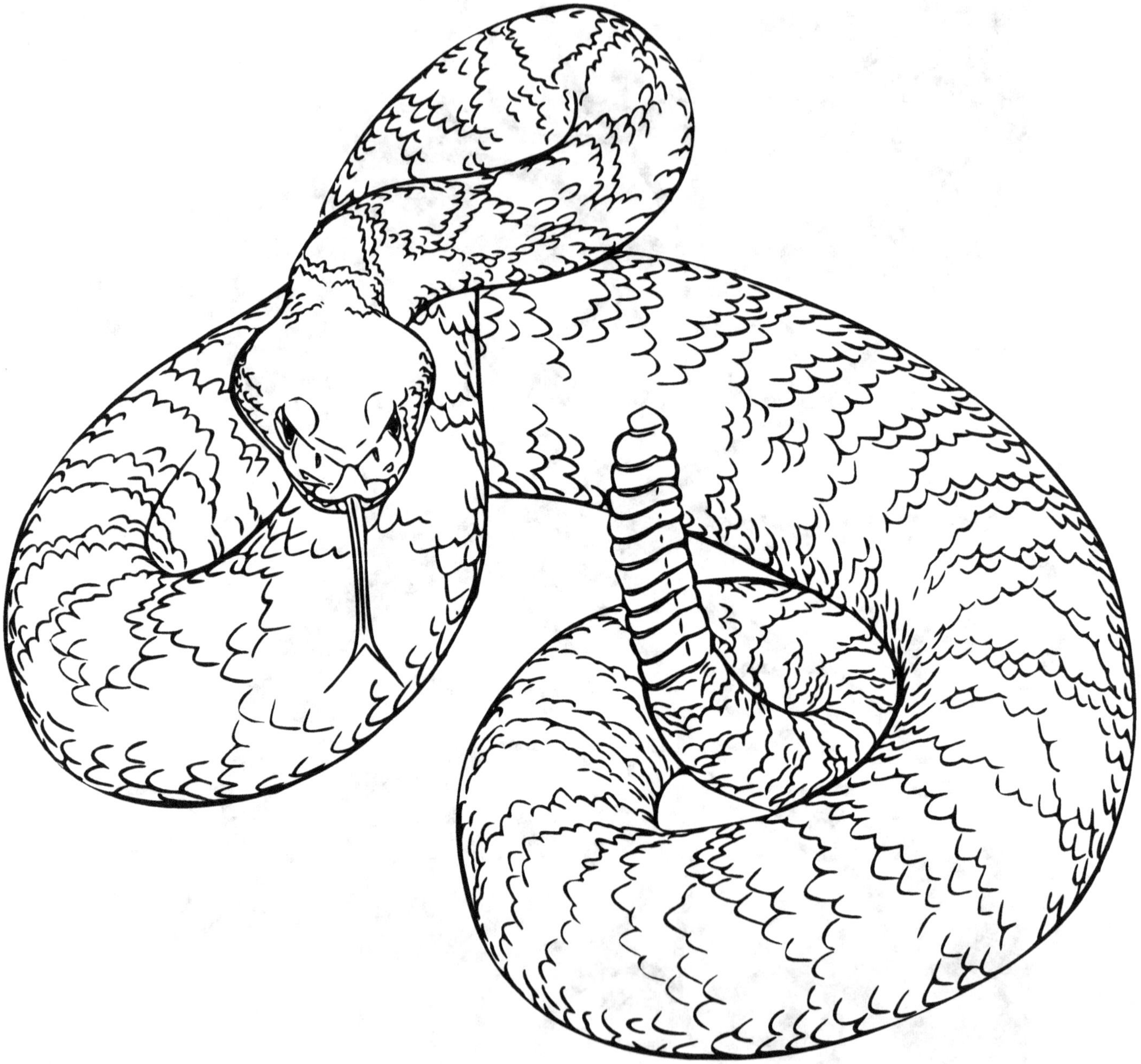

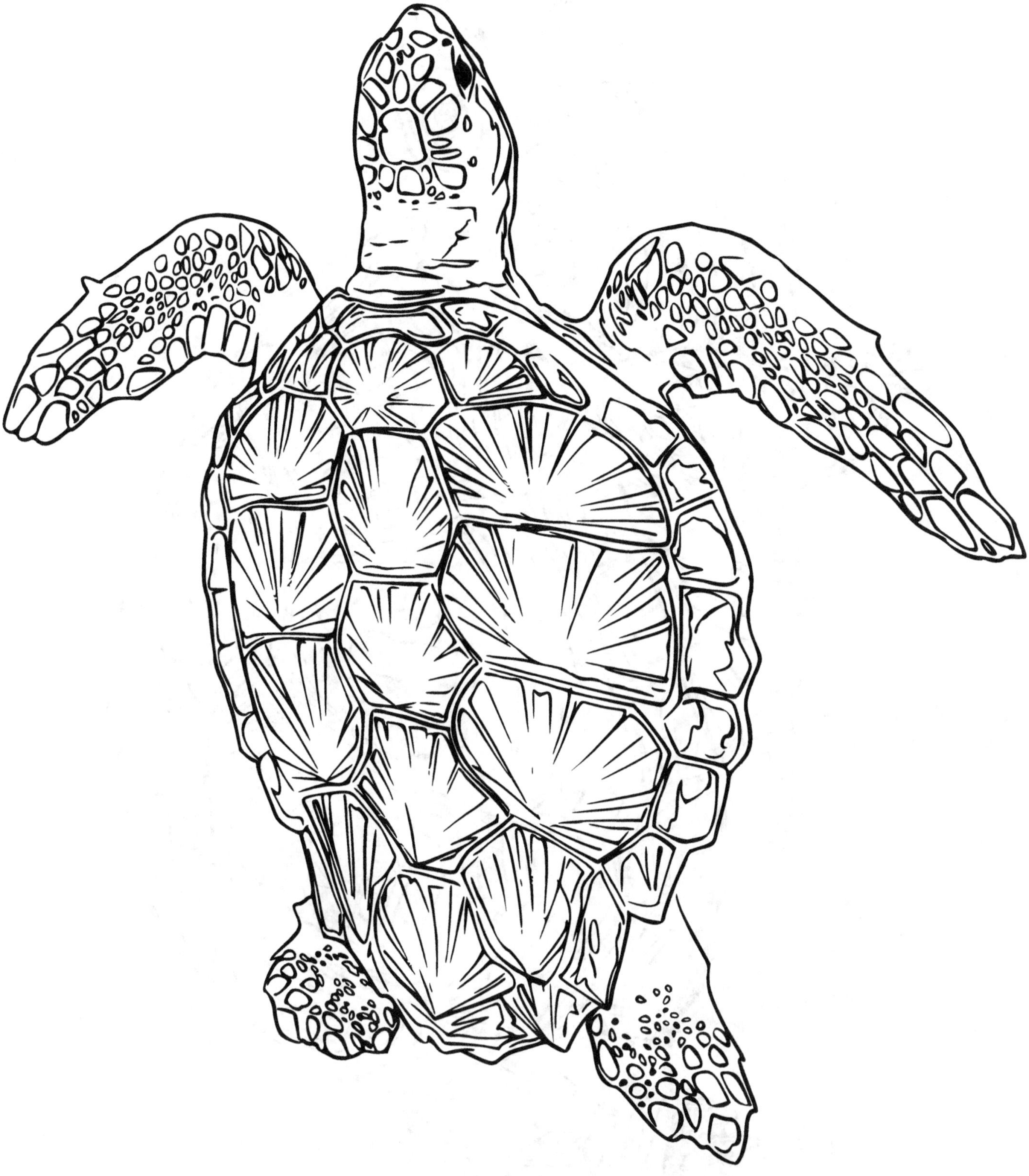

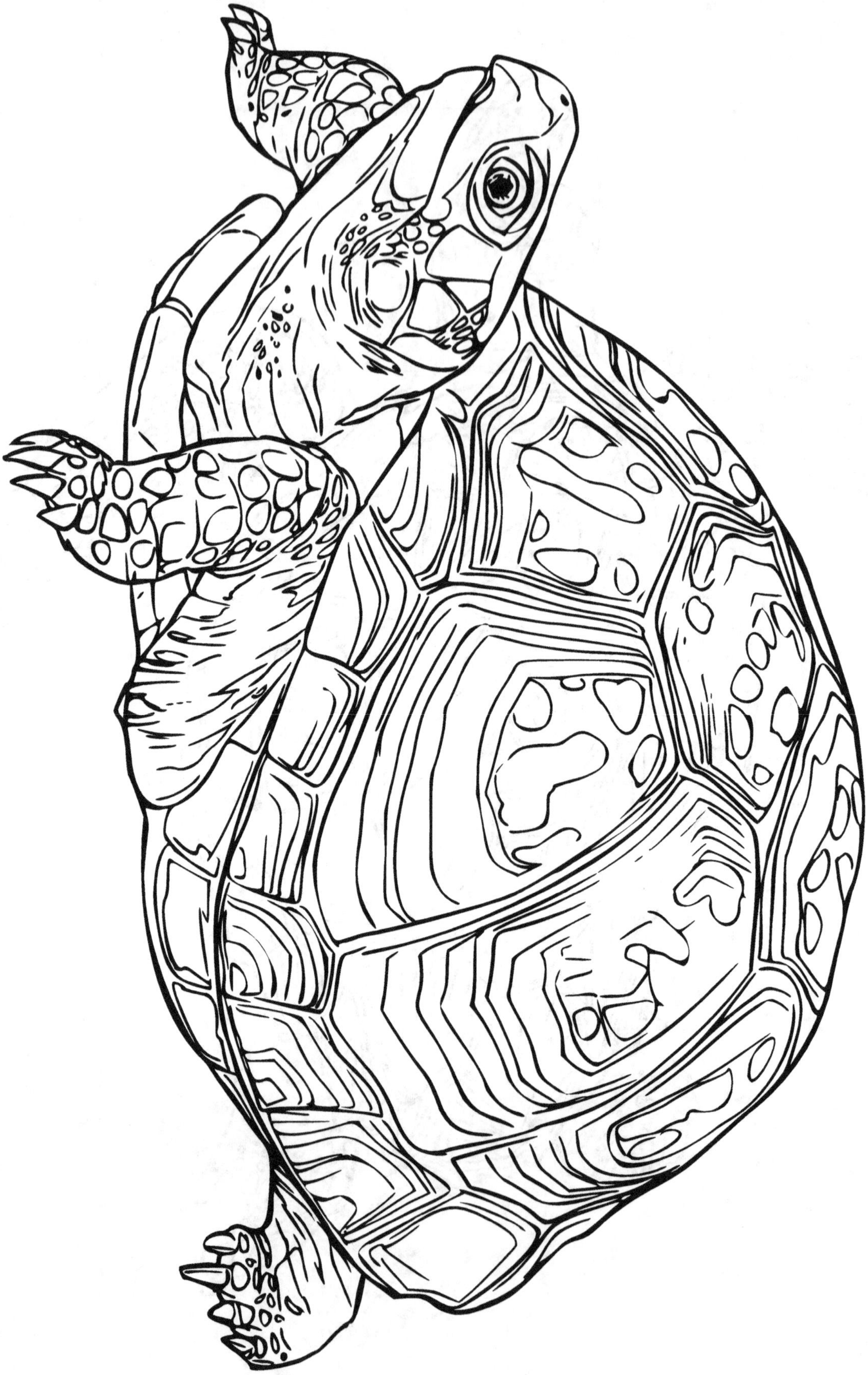

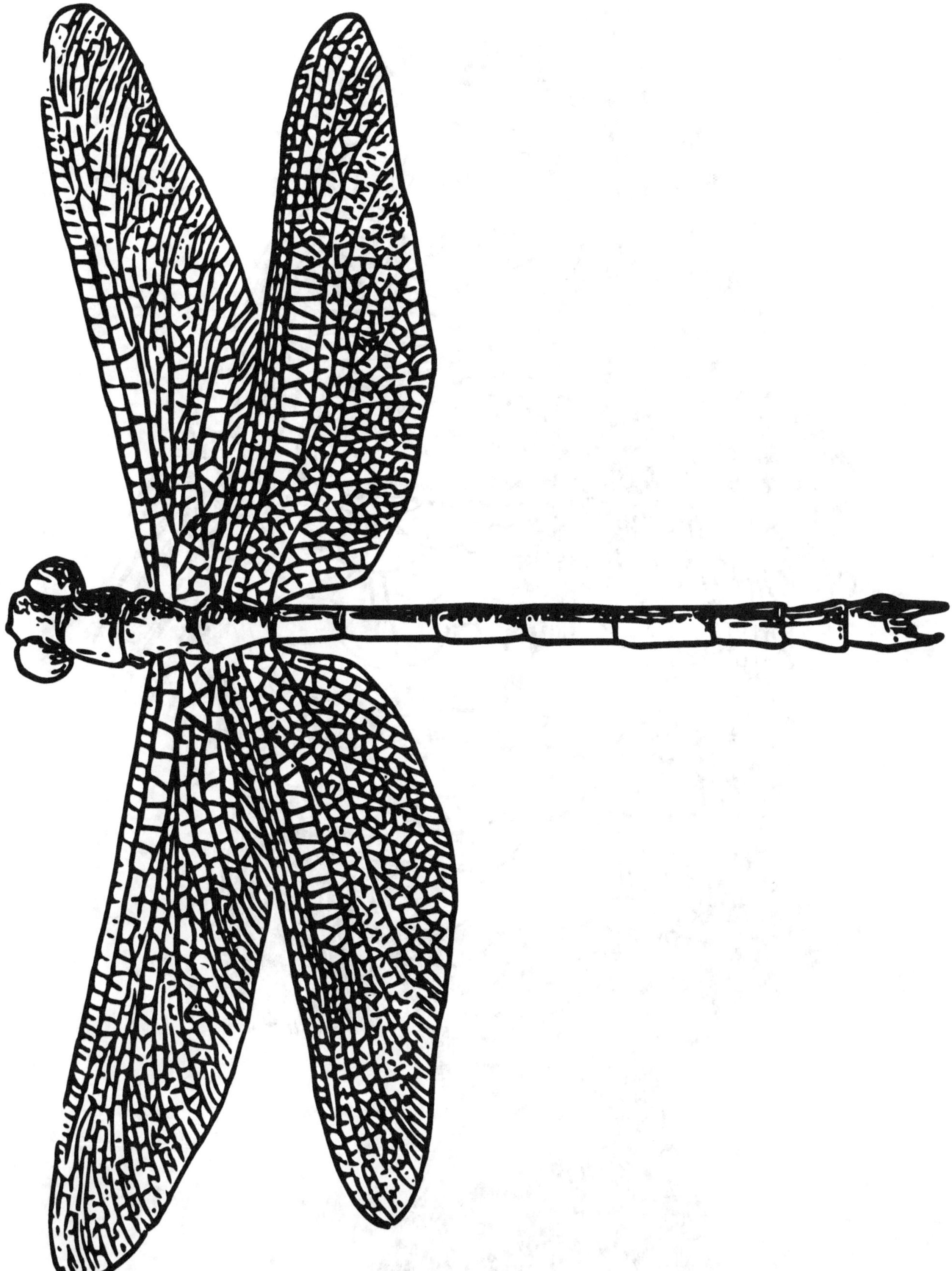

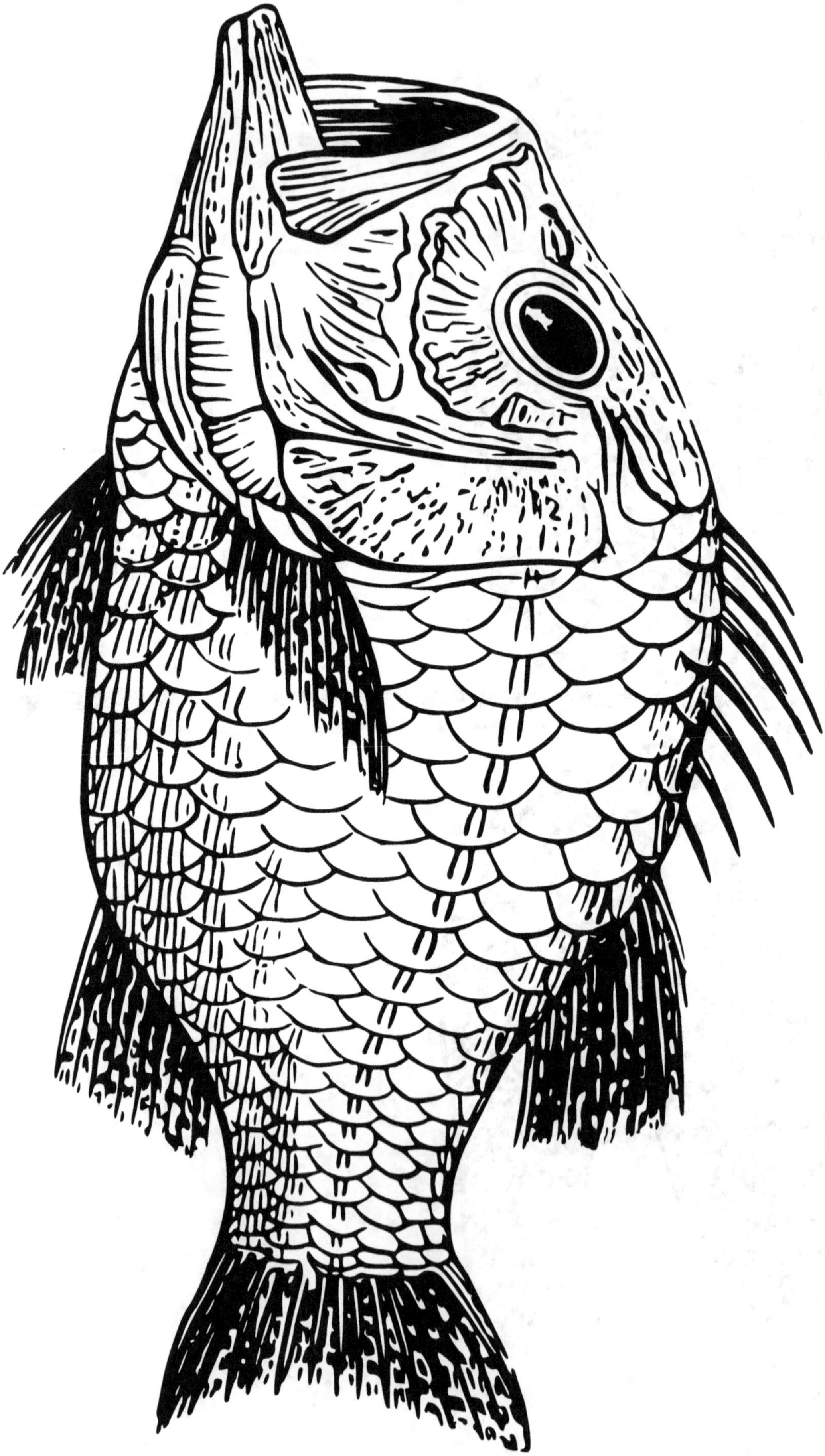

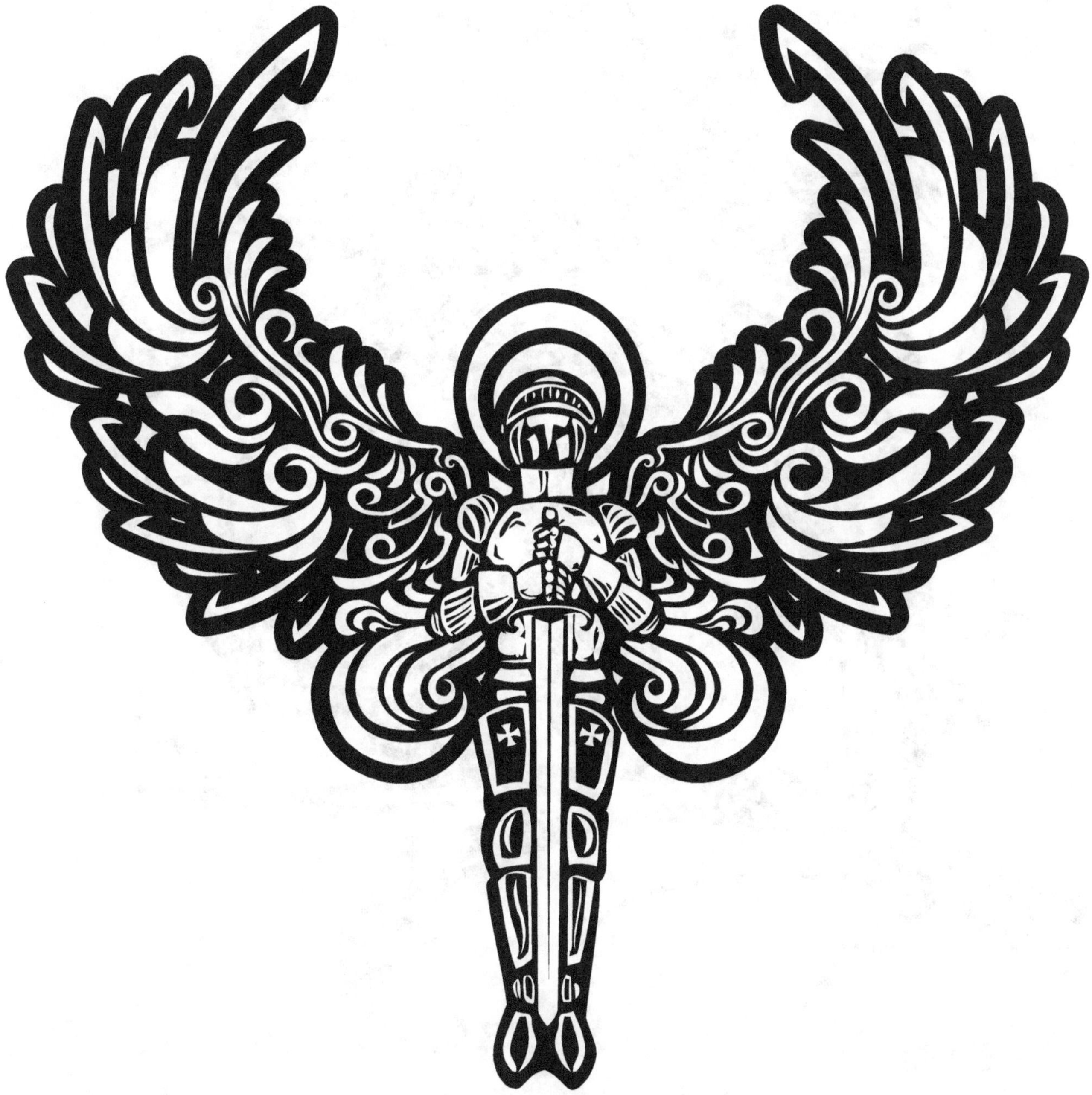

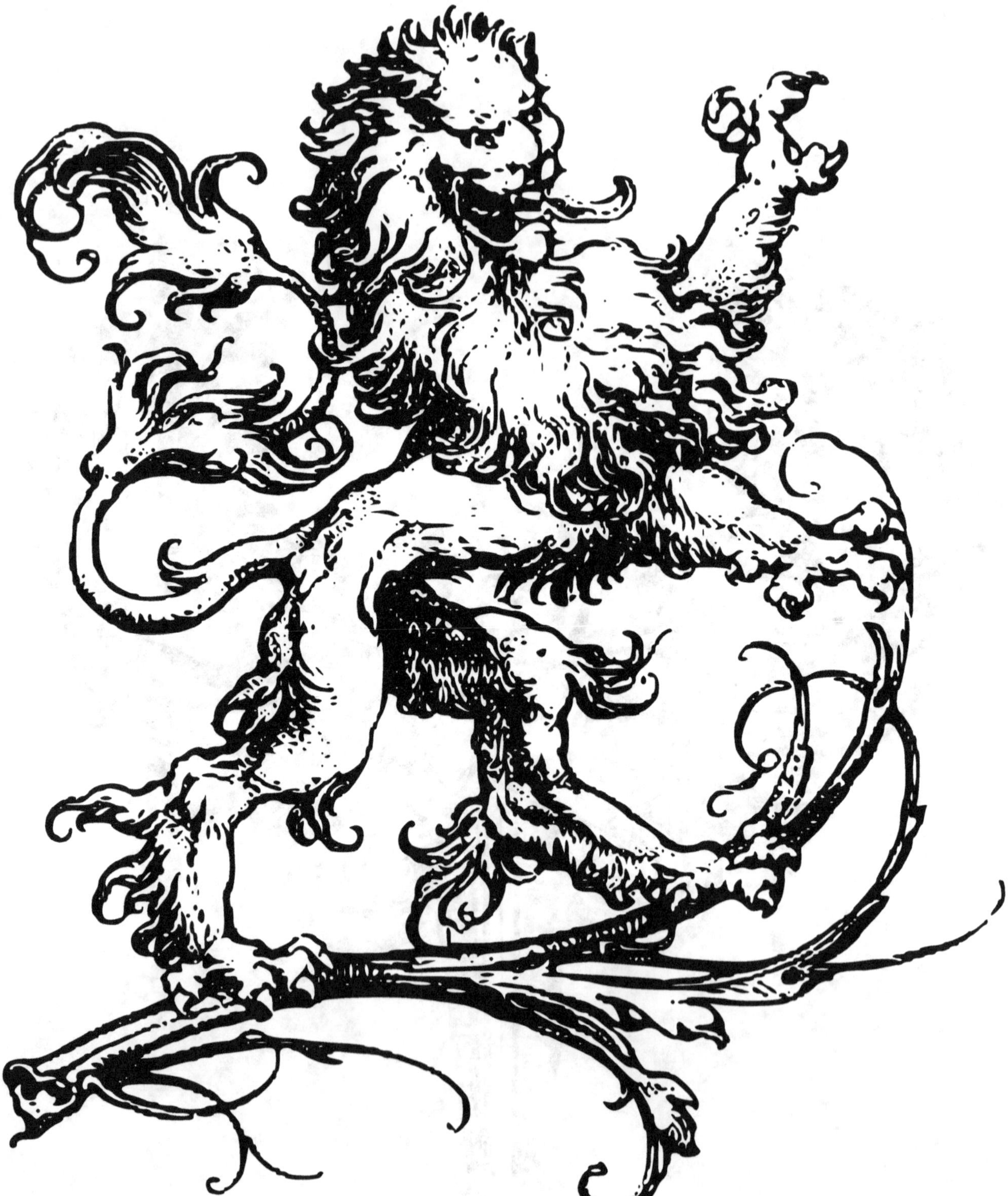

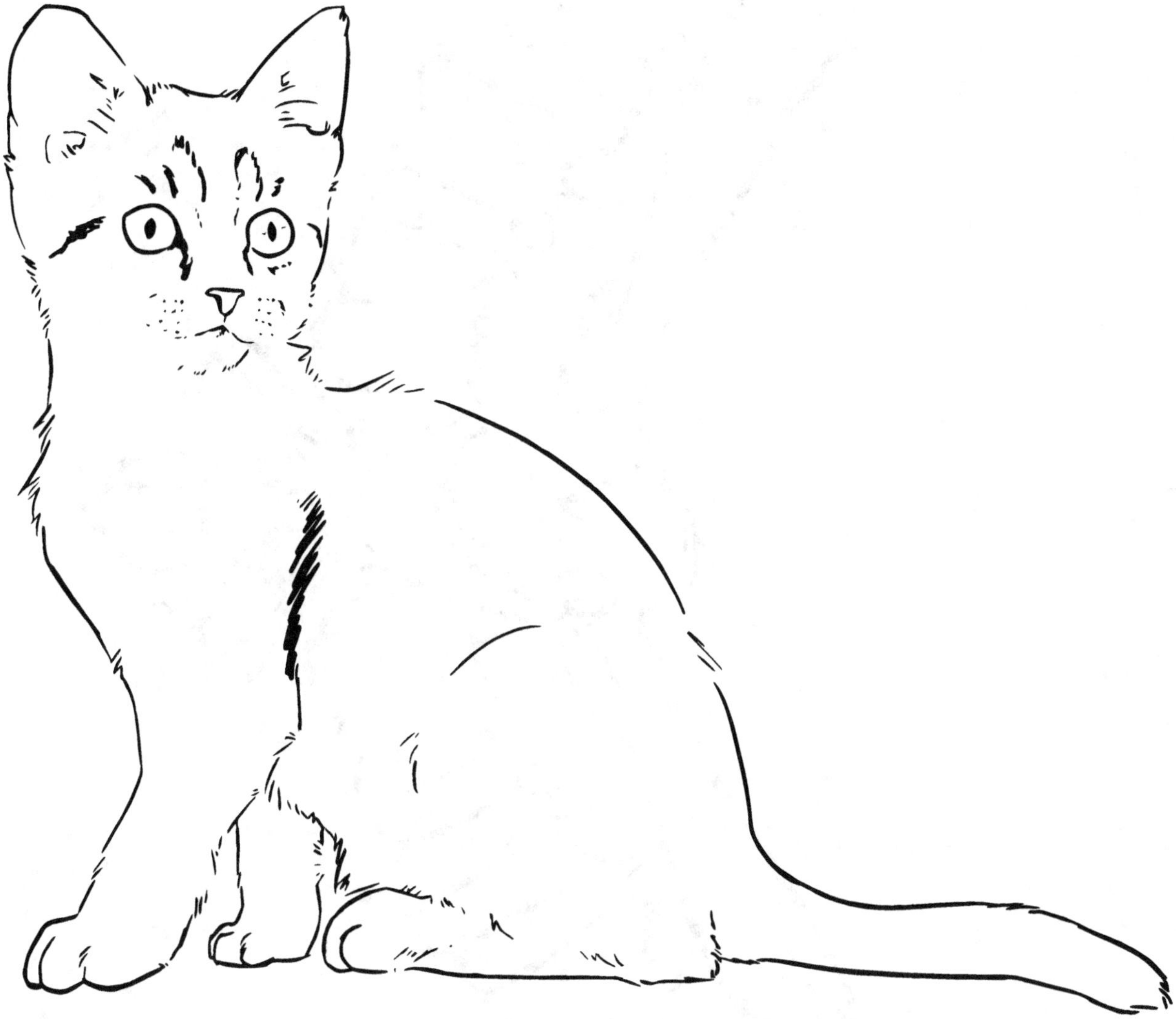

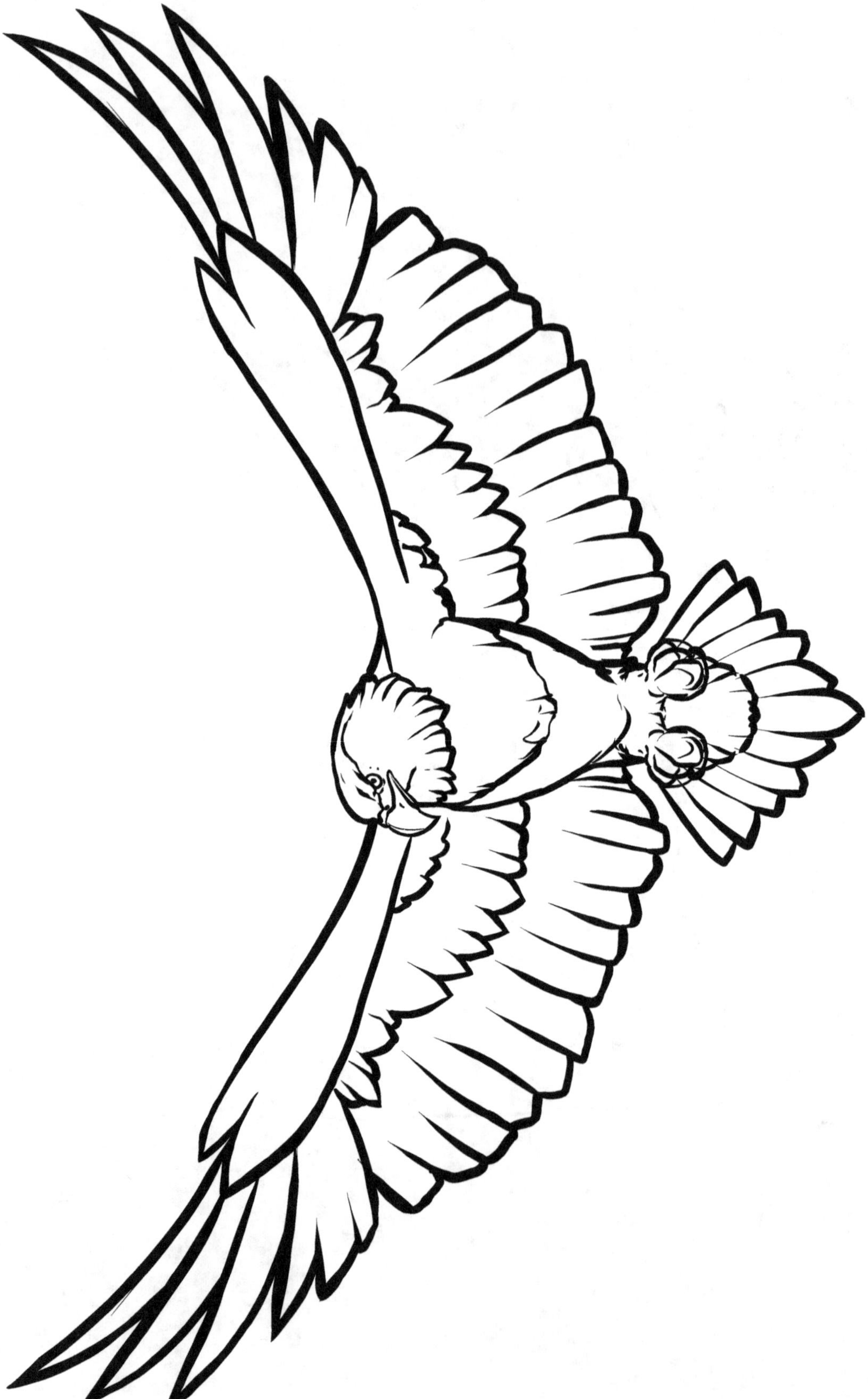

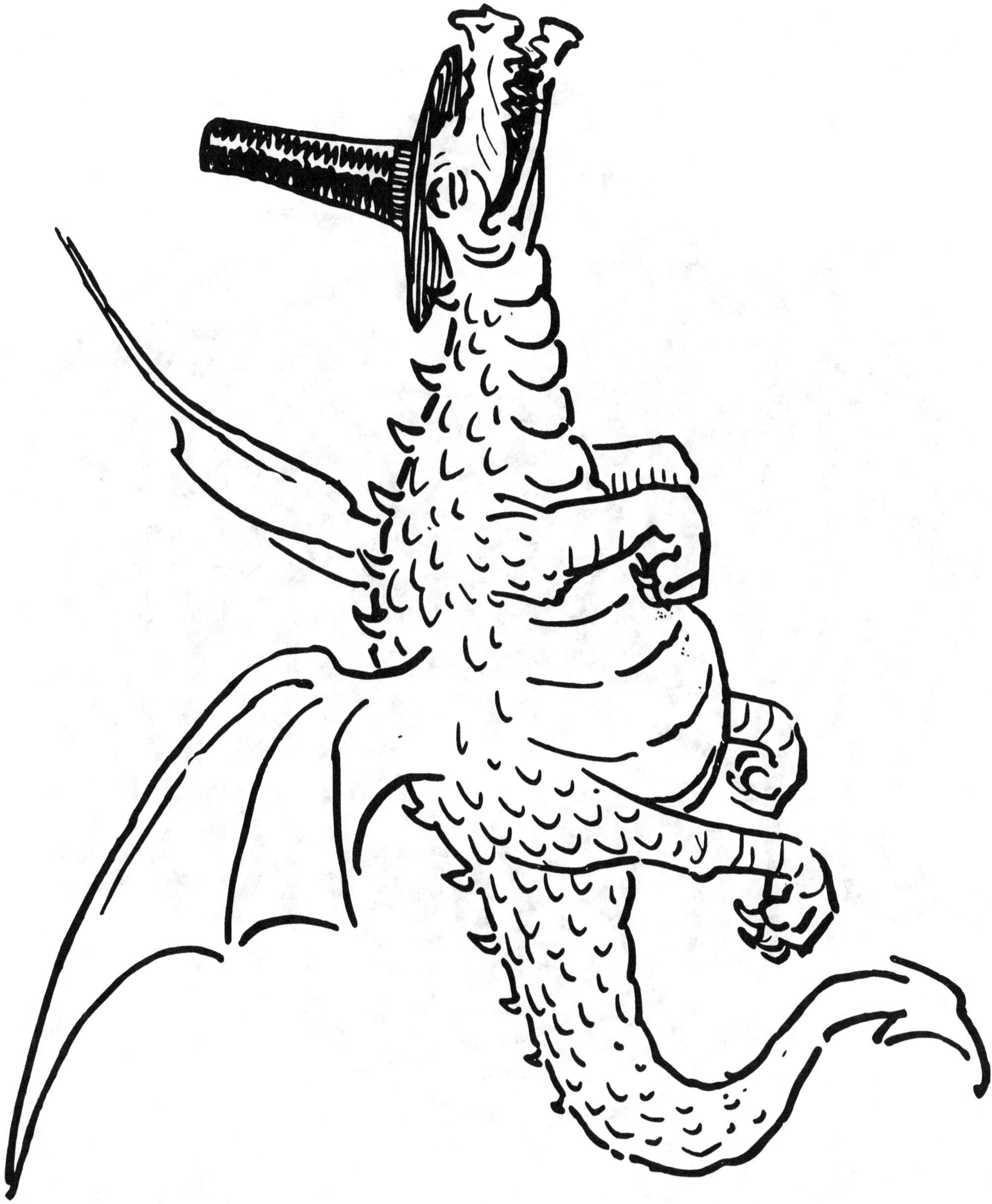

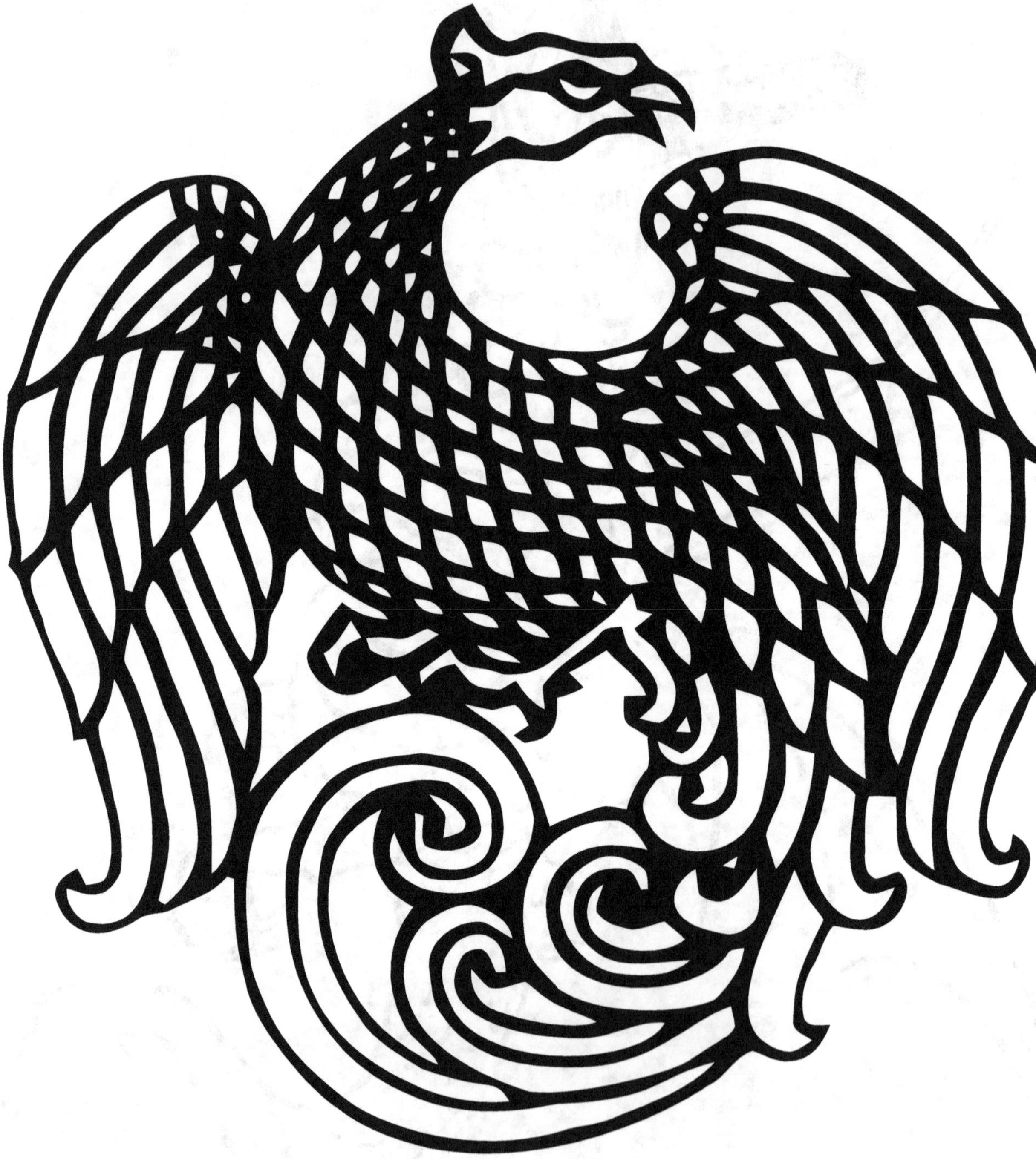

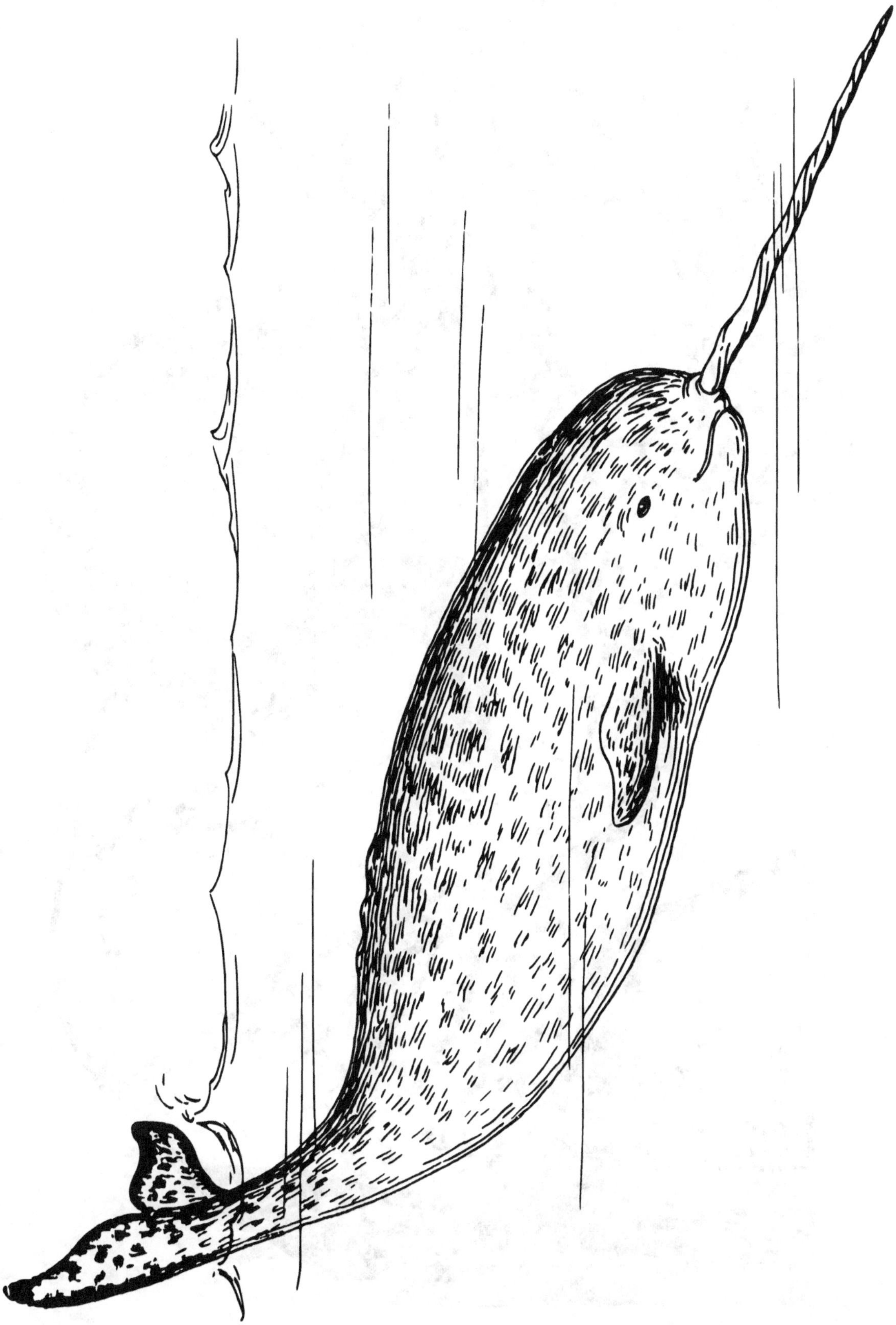

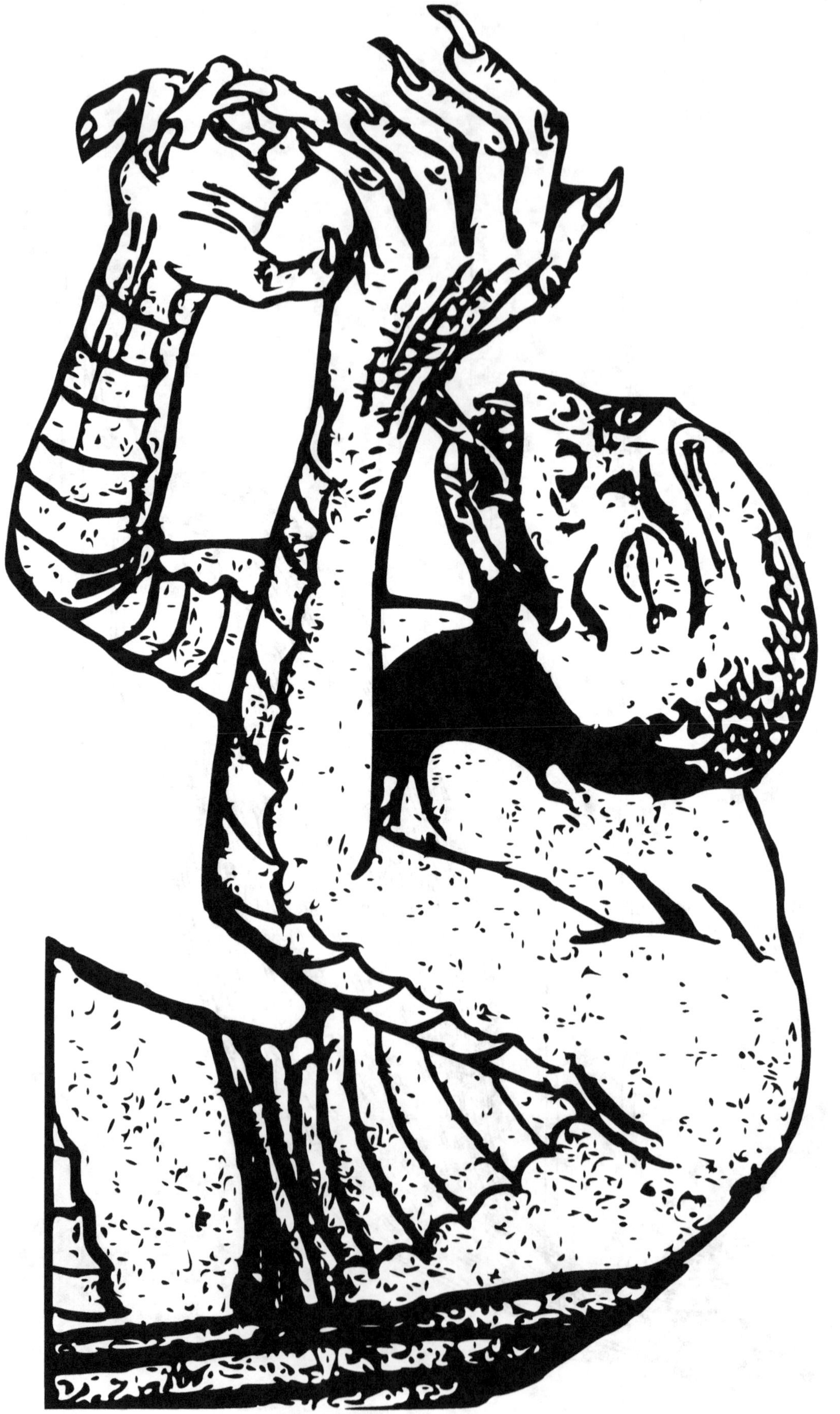

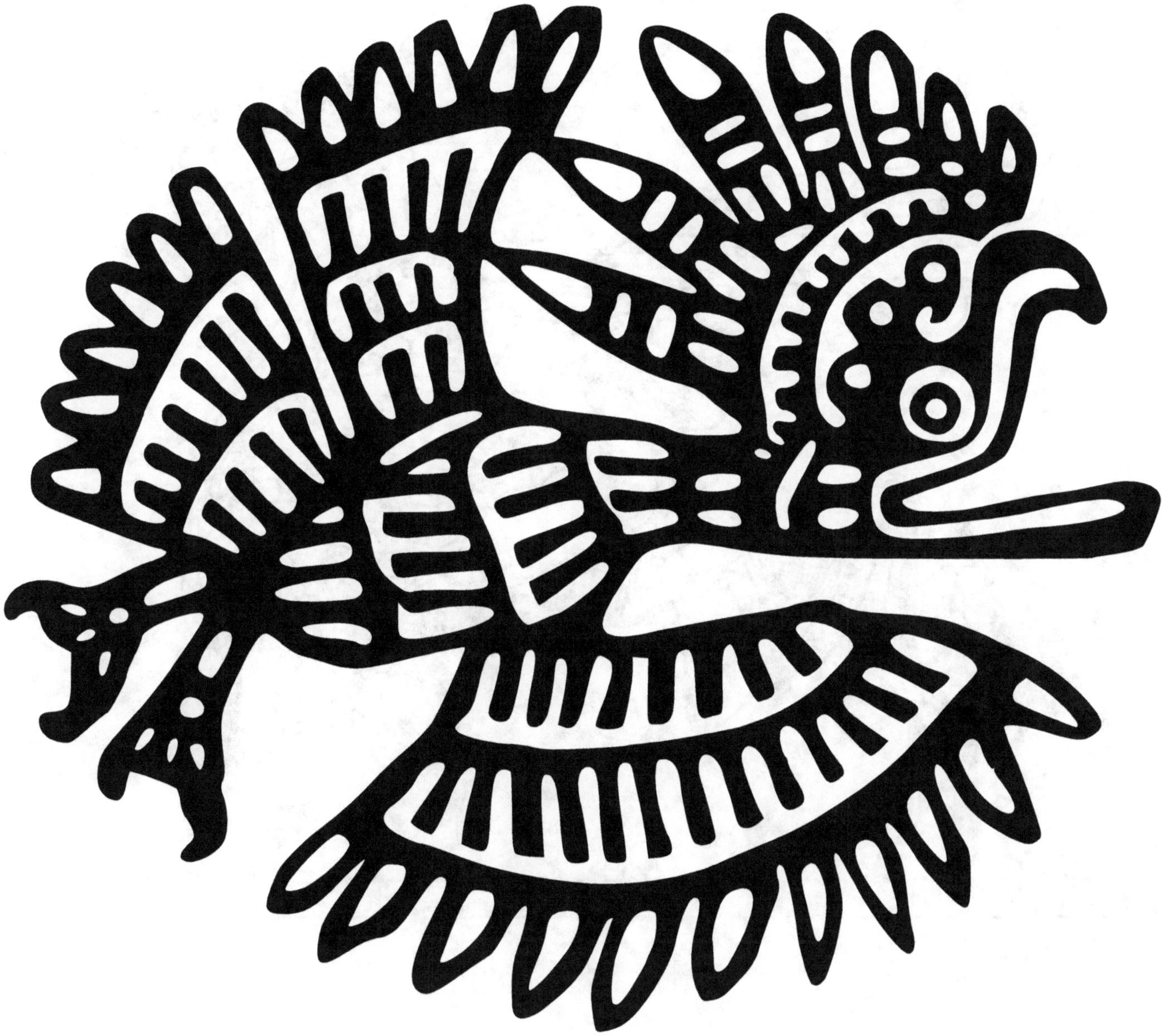

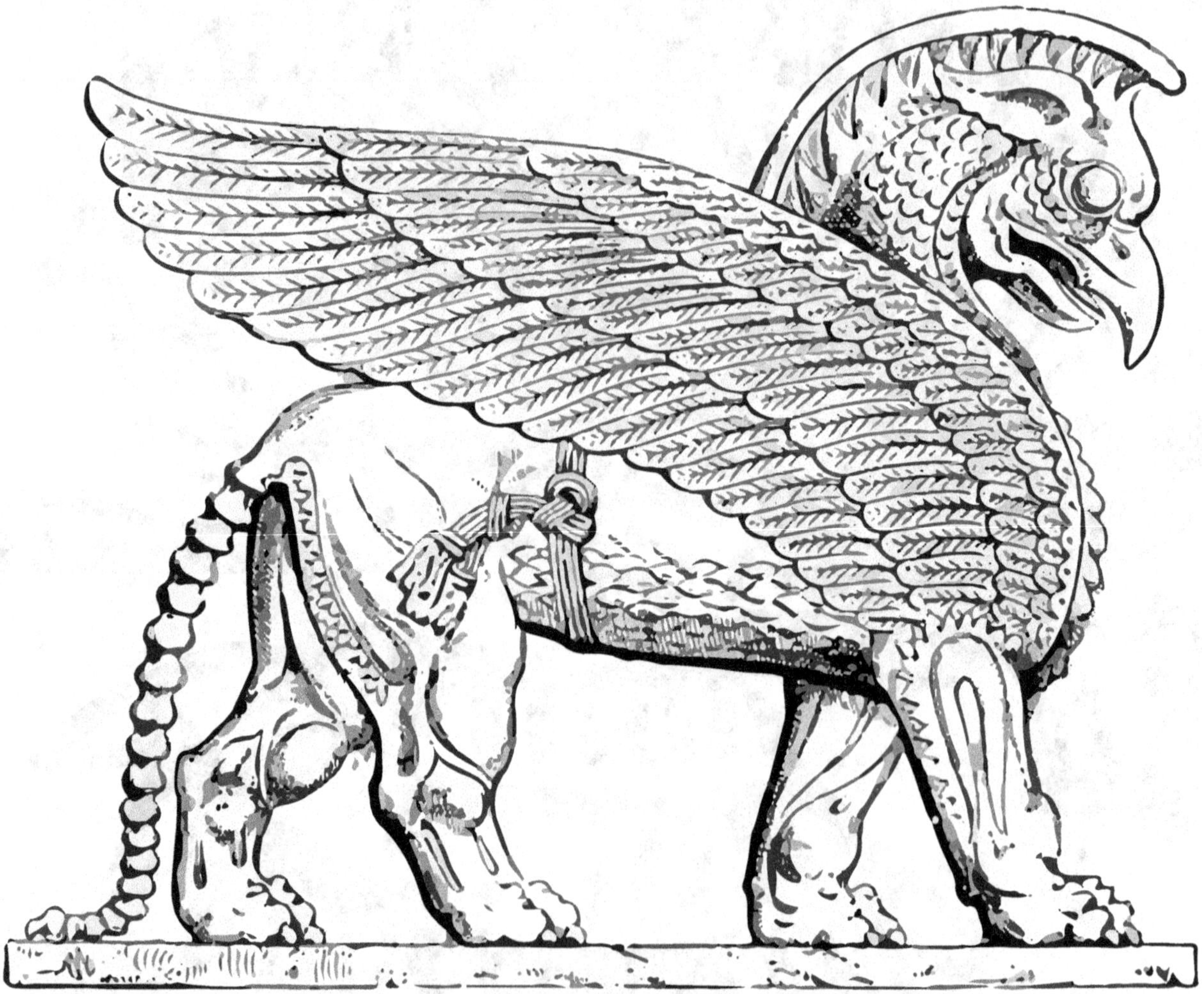

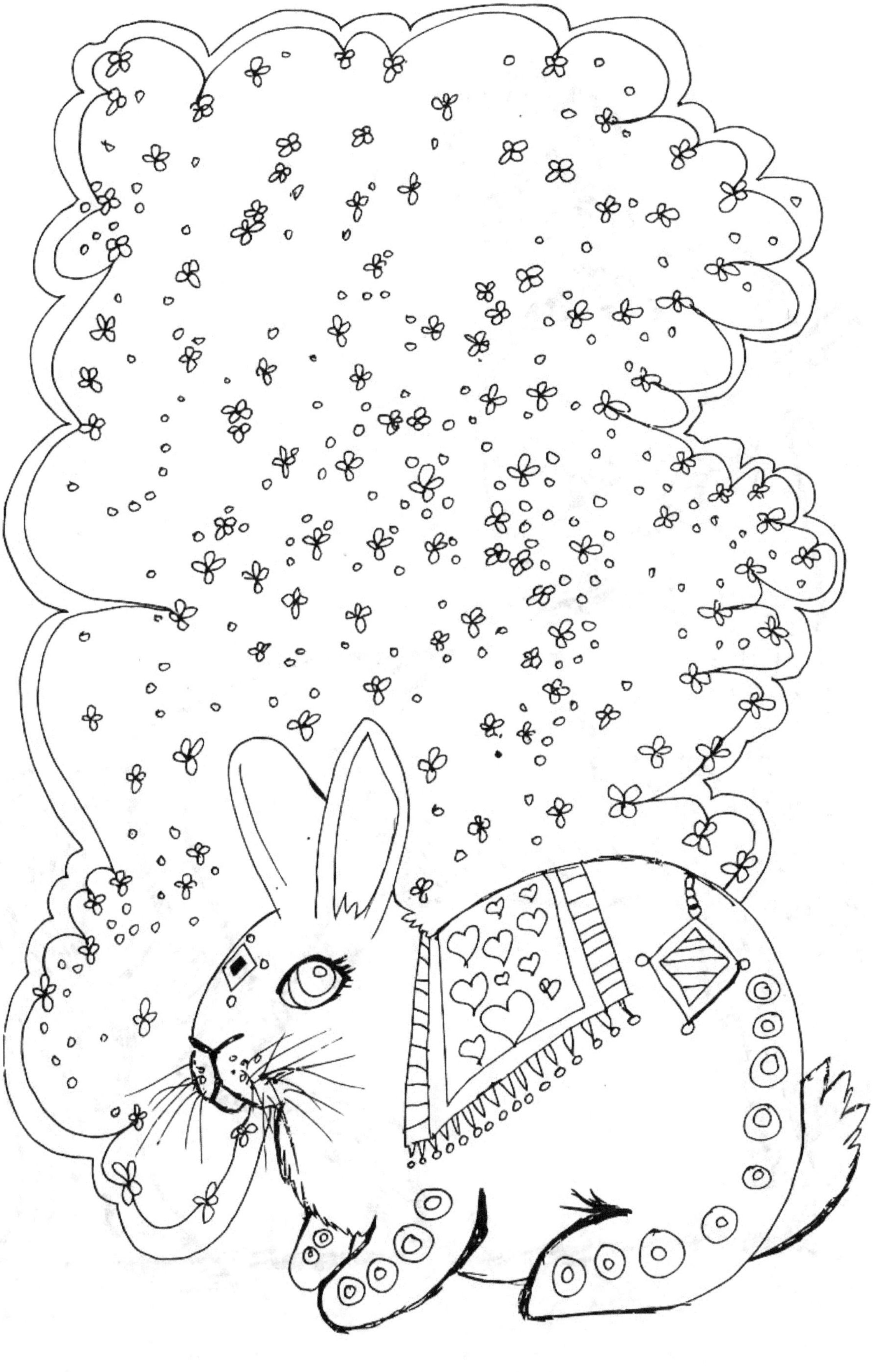

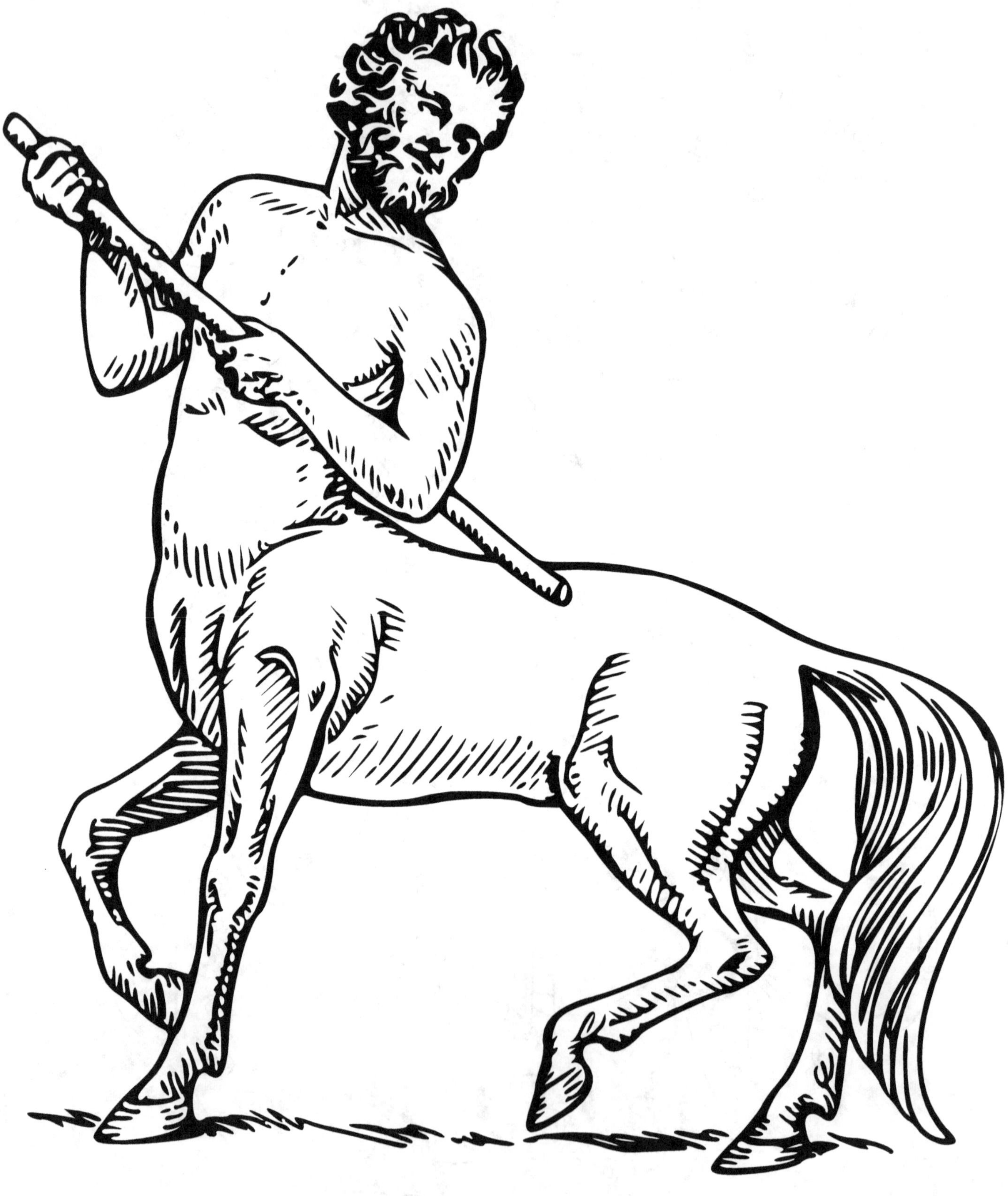

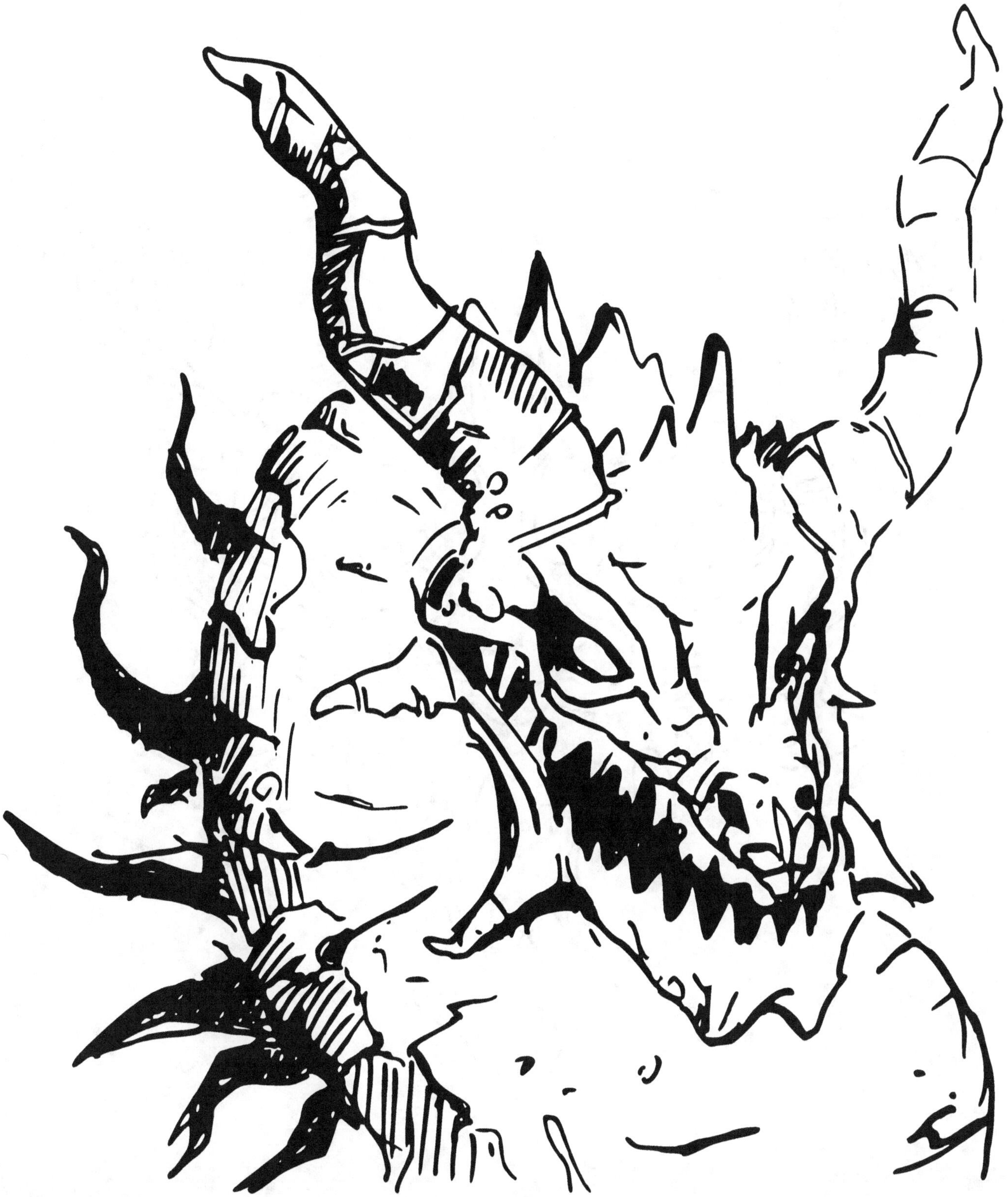

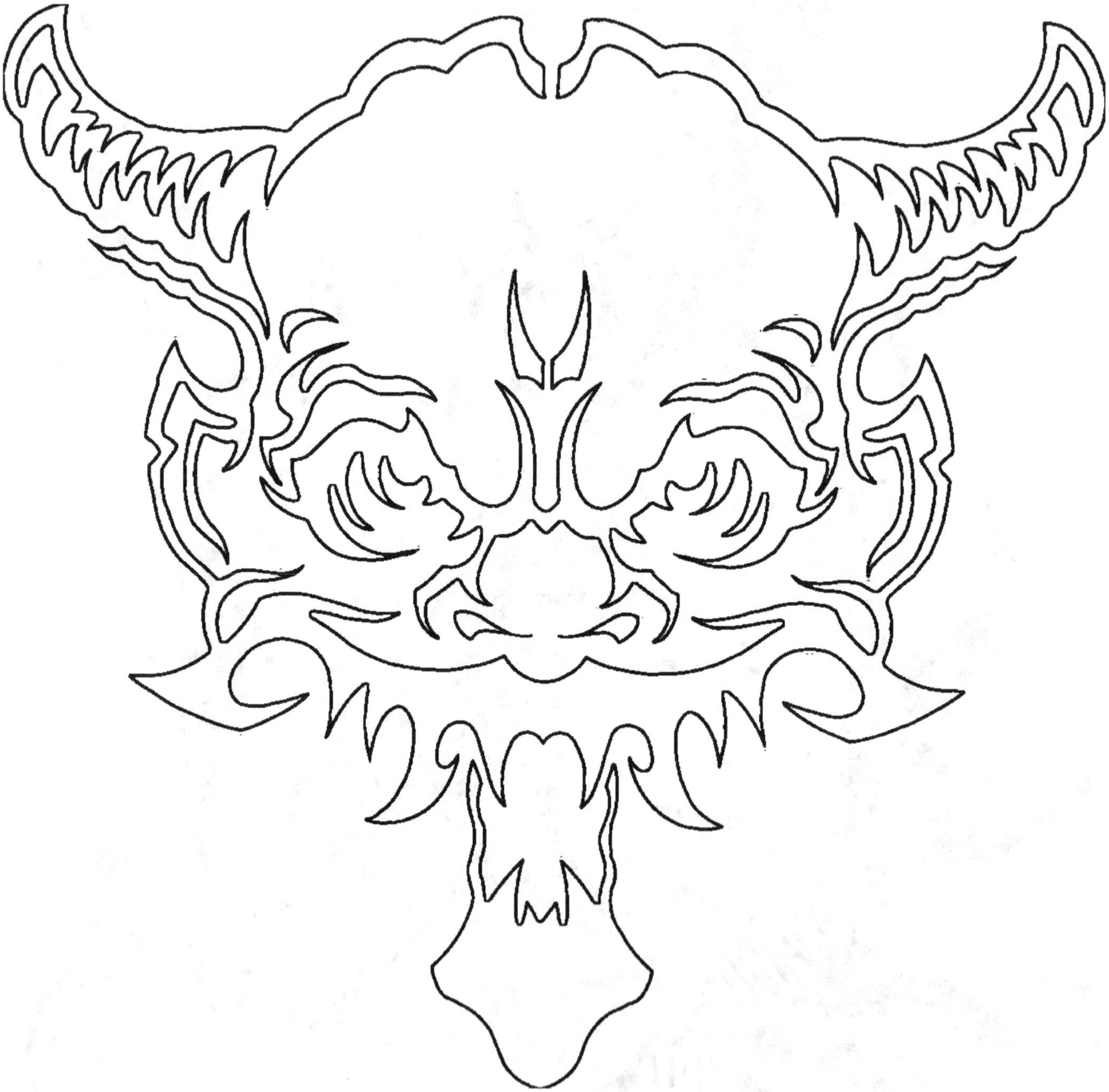

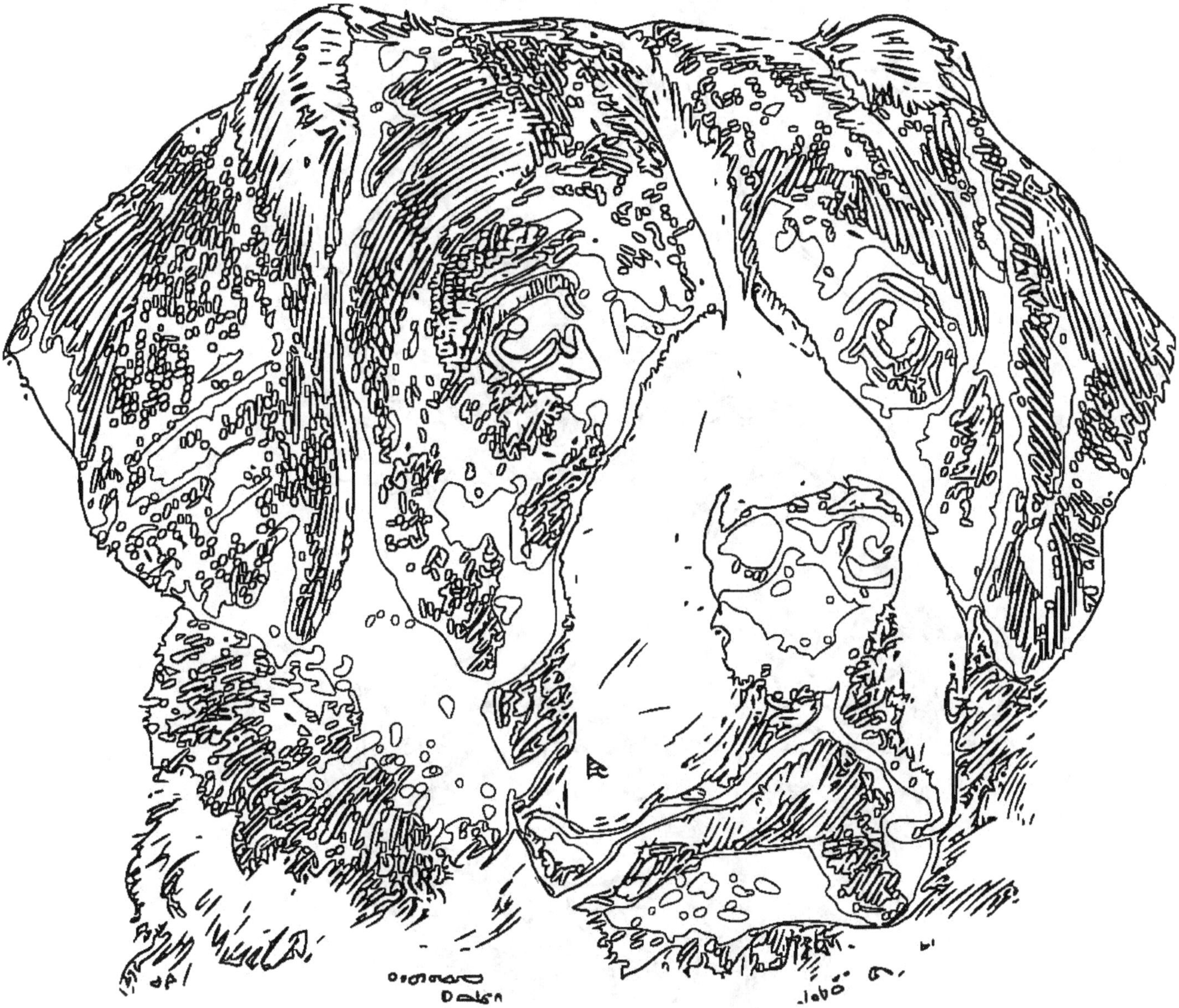

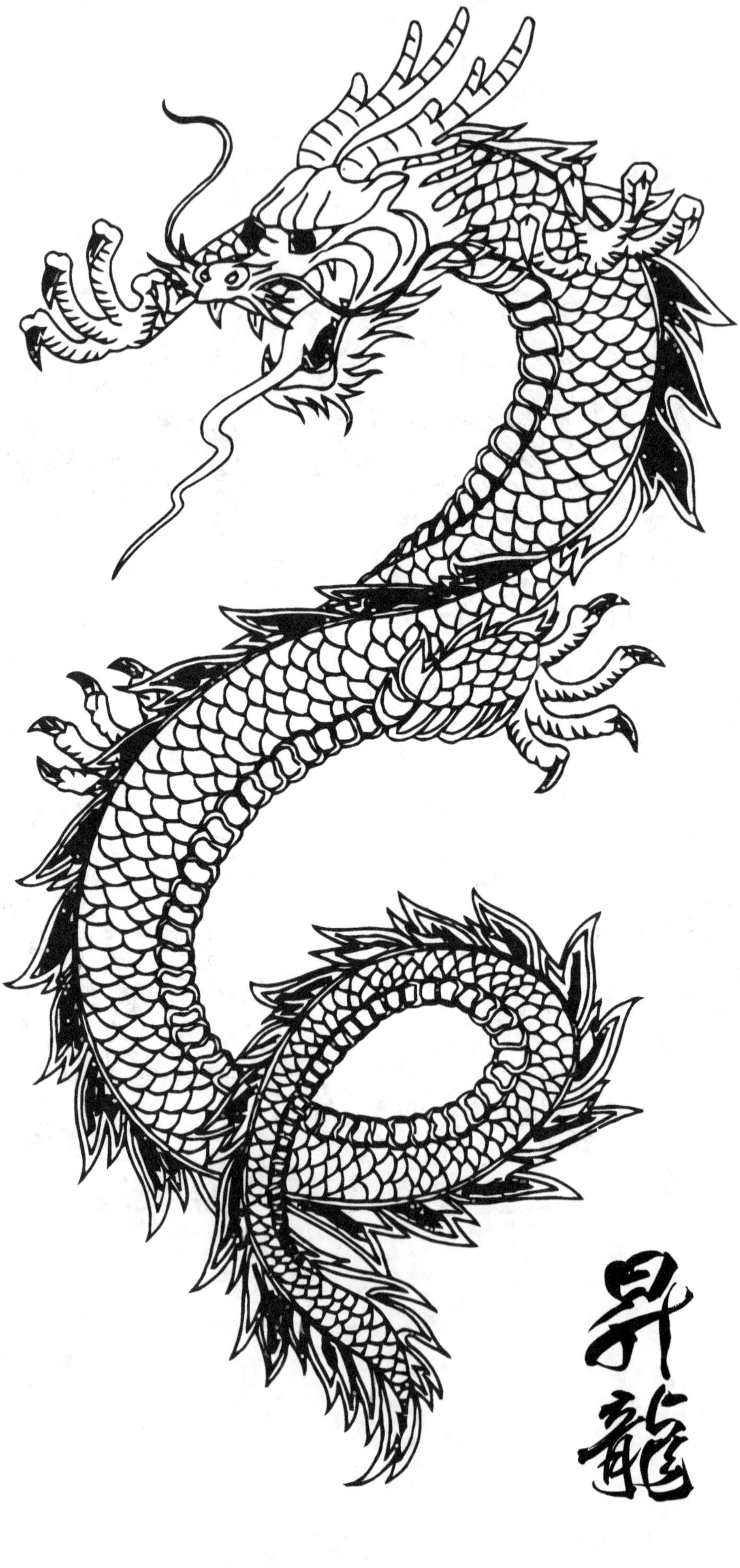
昇龍

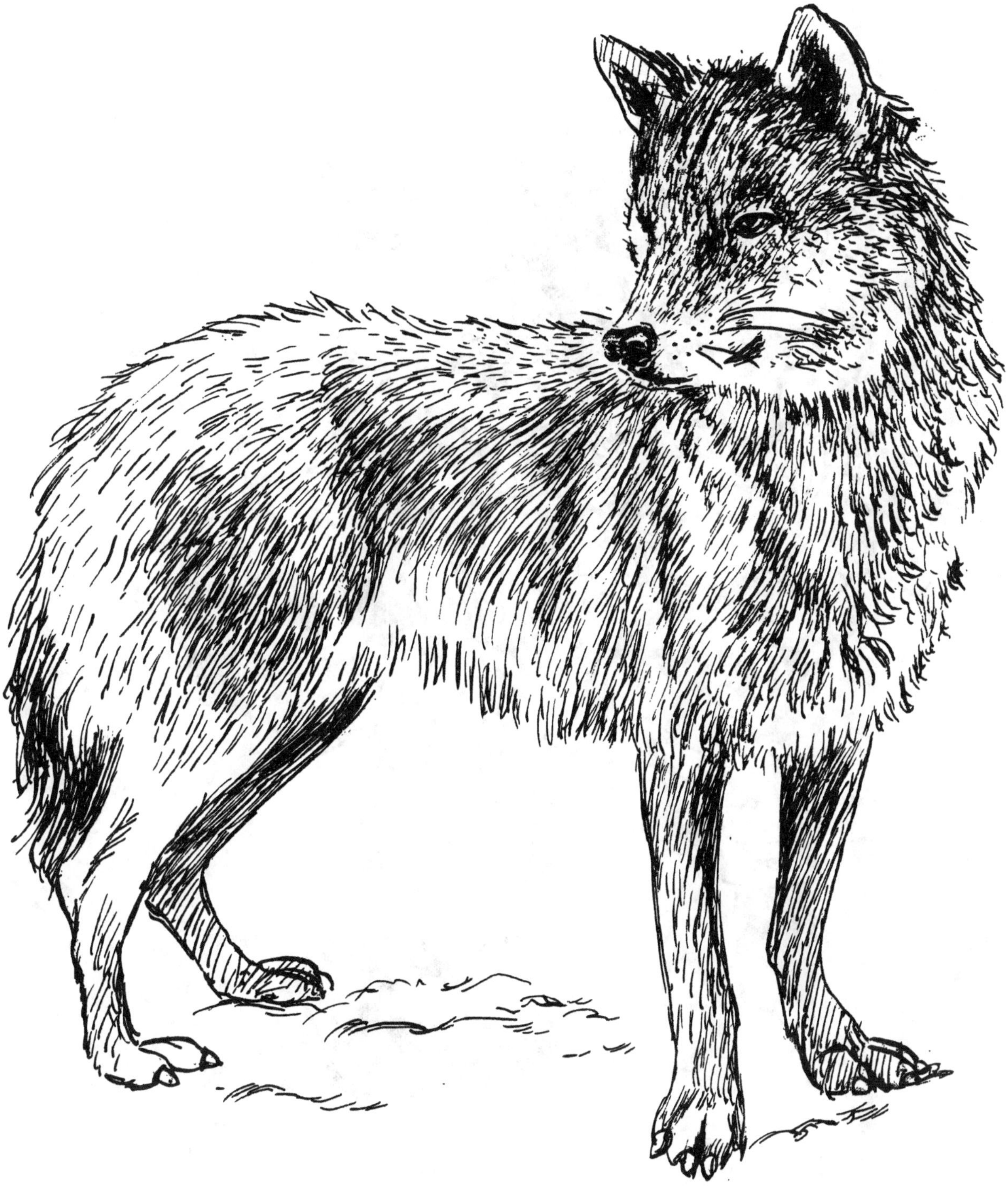

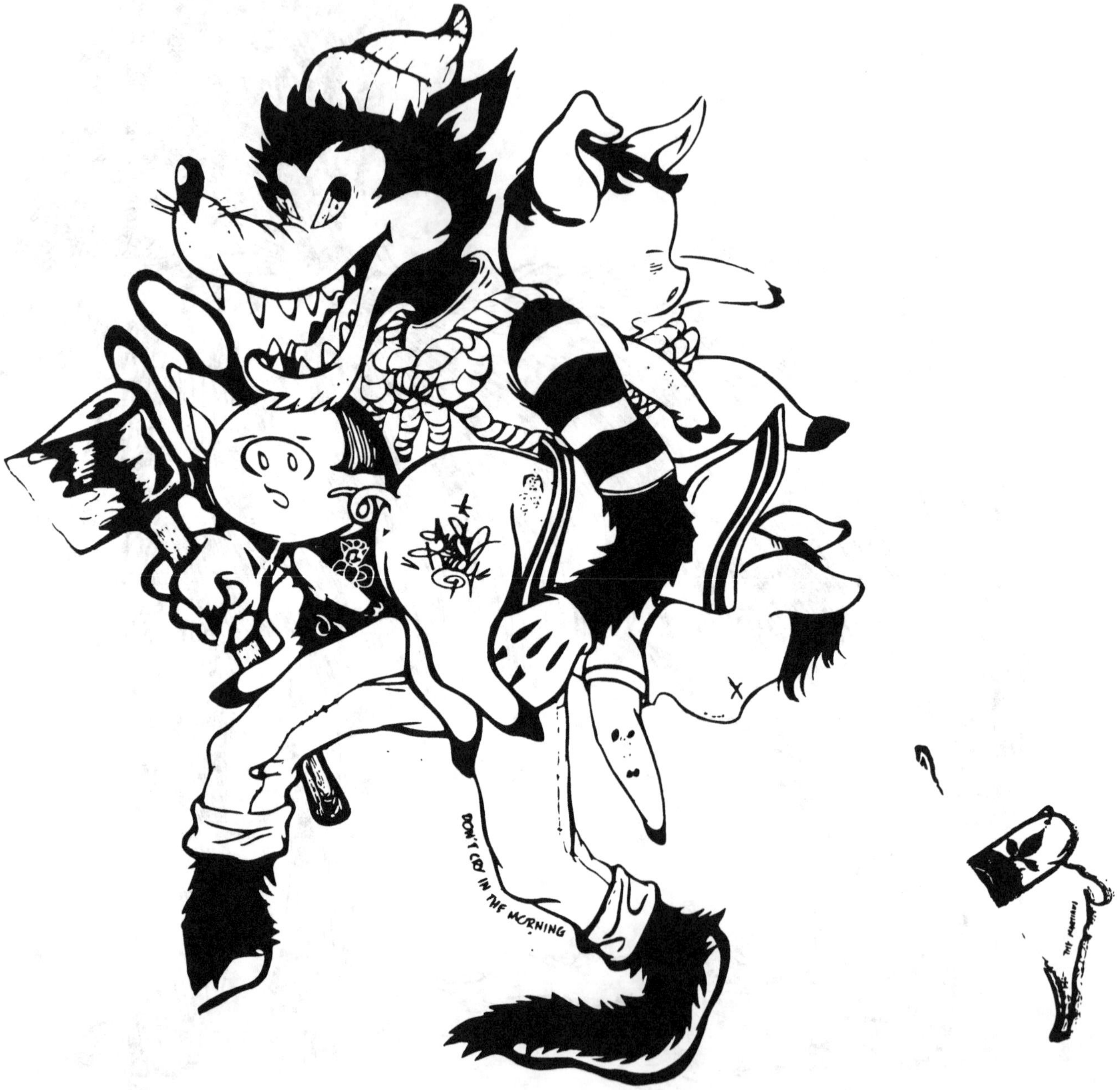
DON'T CRY IN THE MORNING

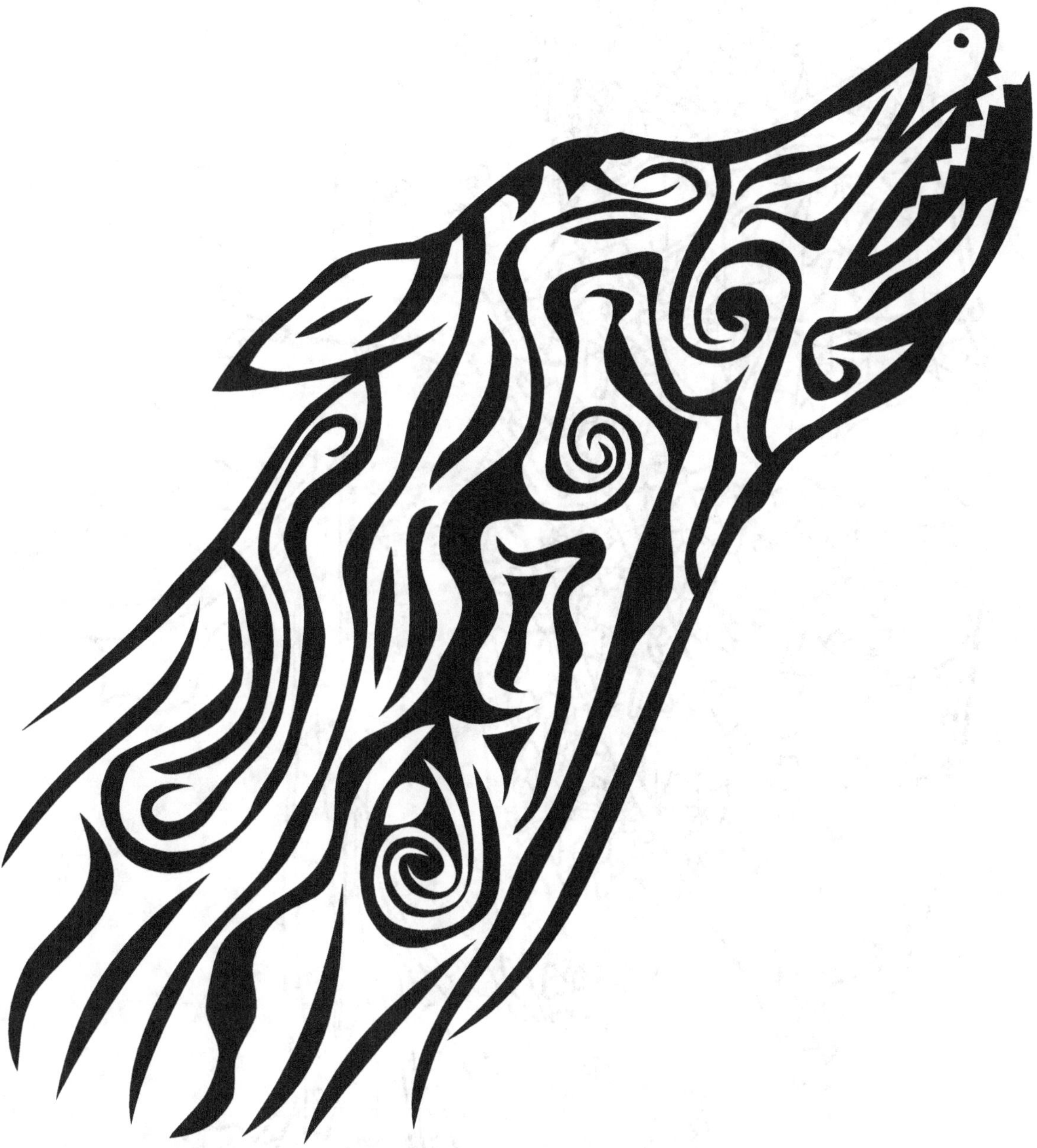

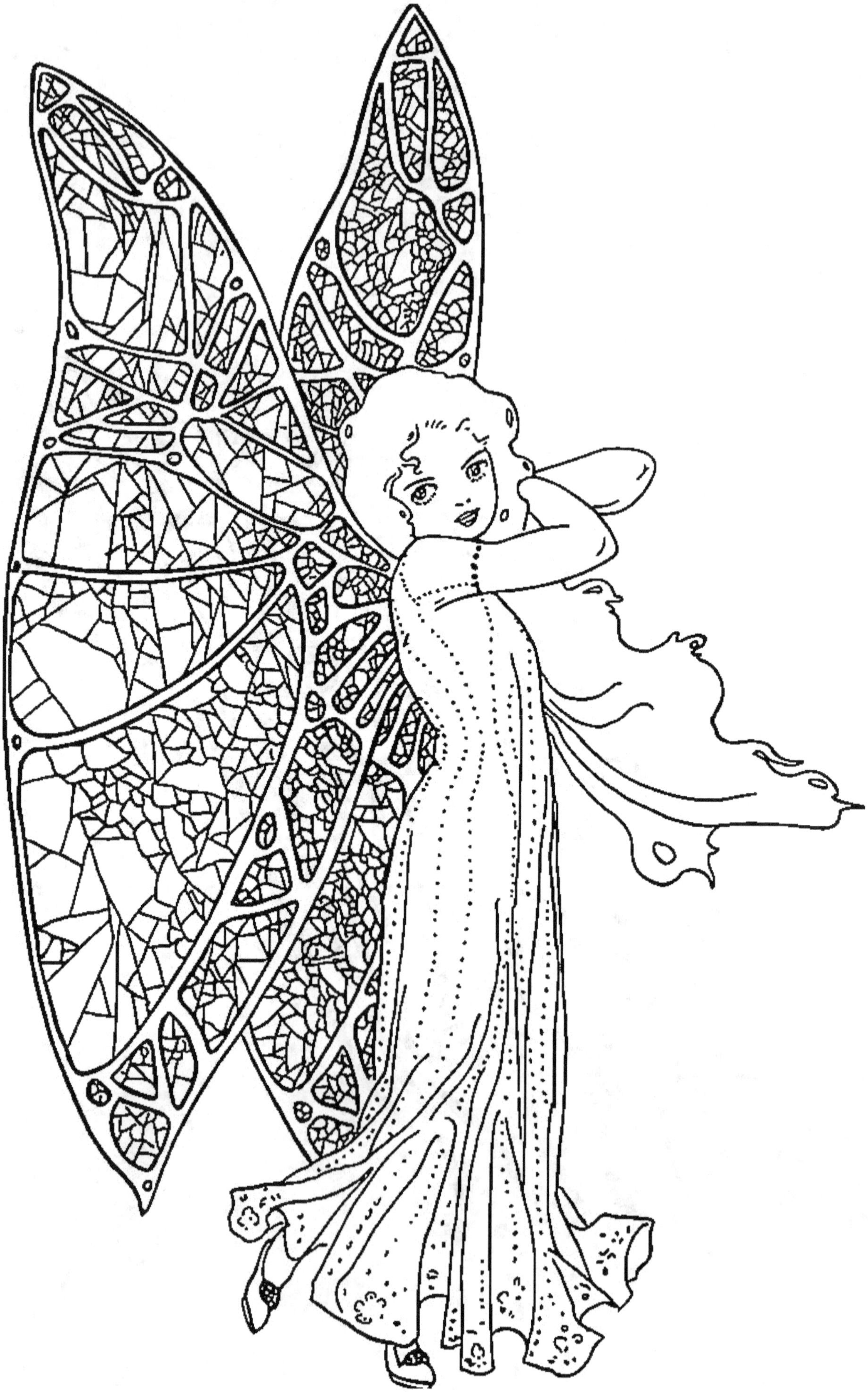

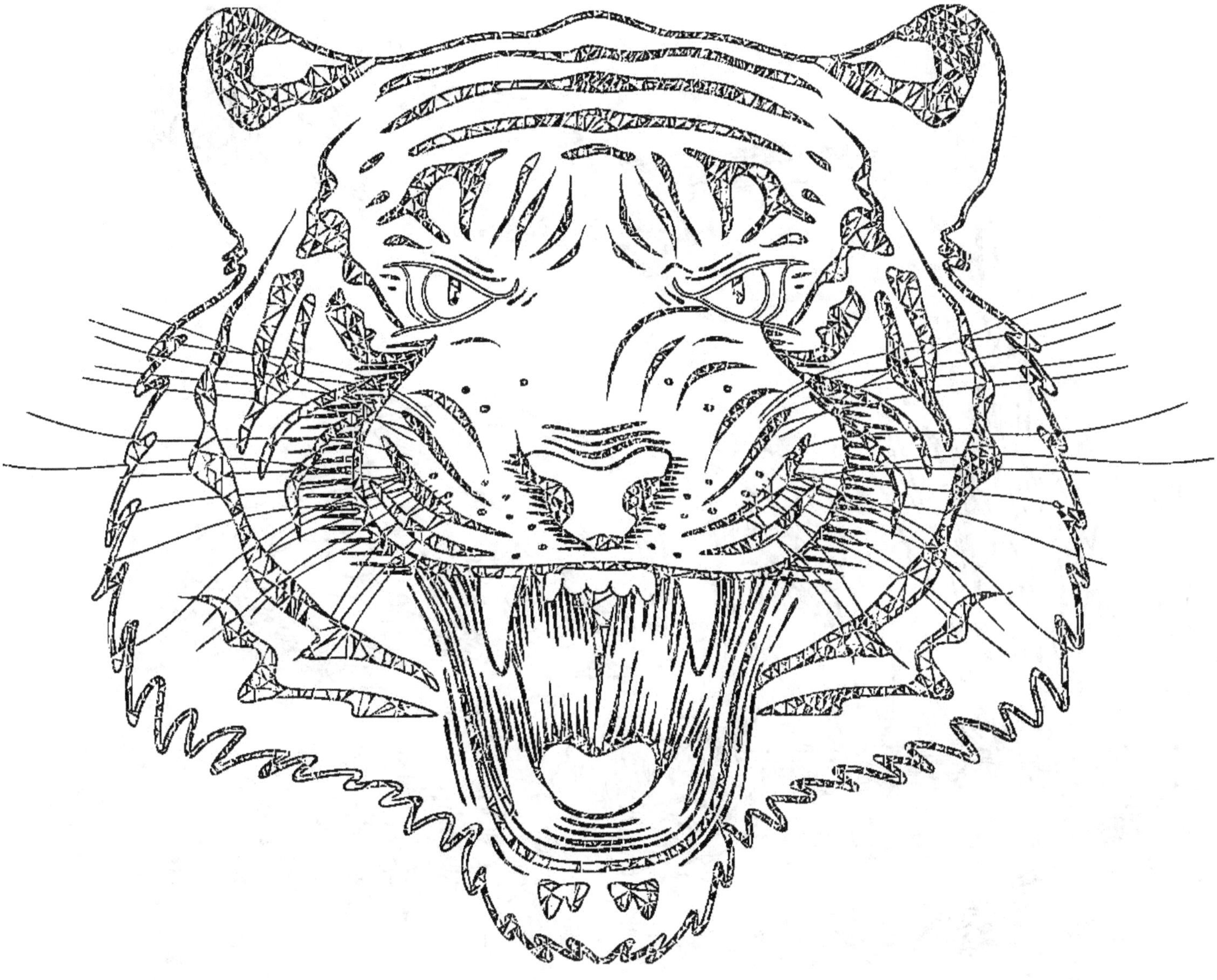

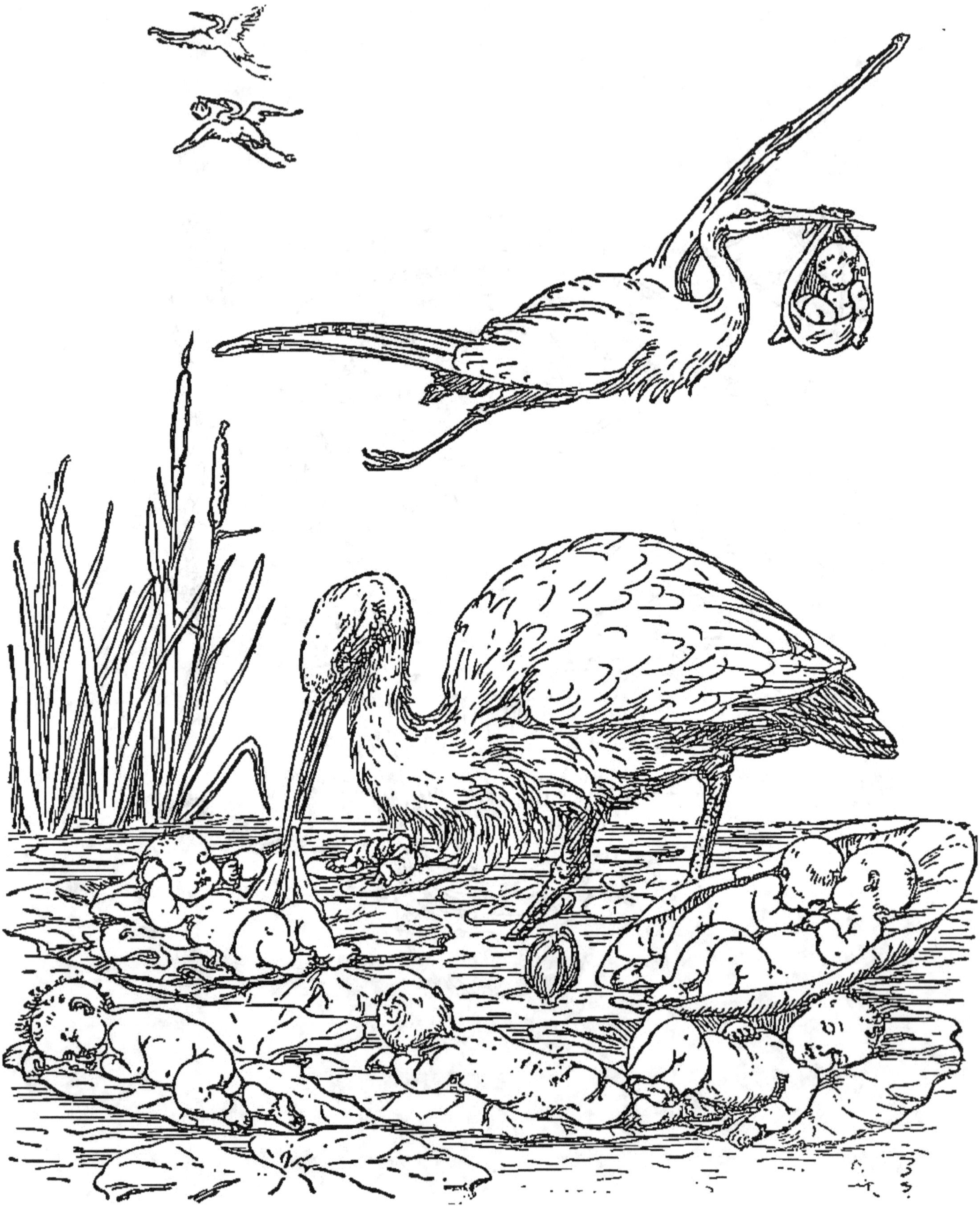

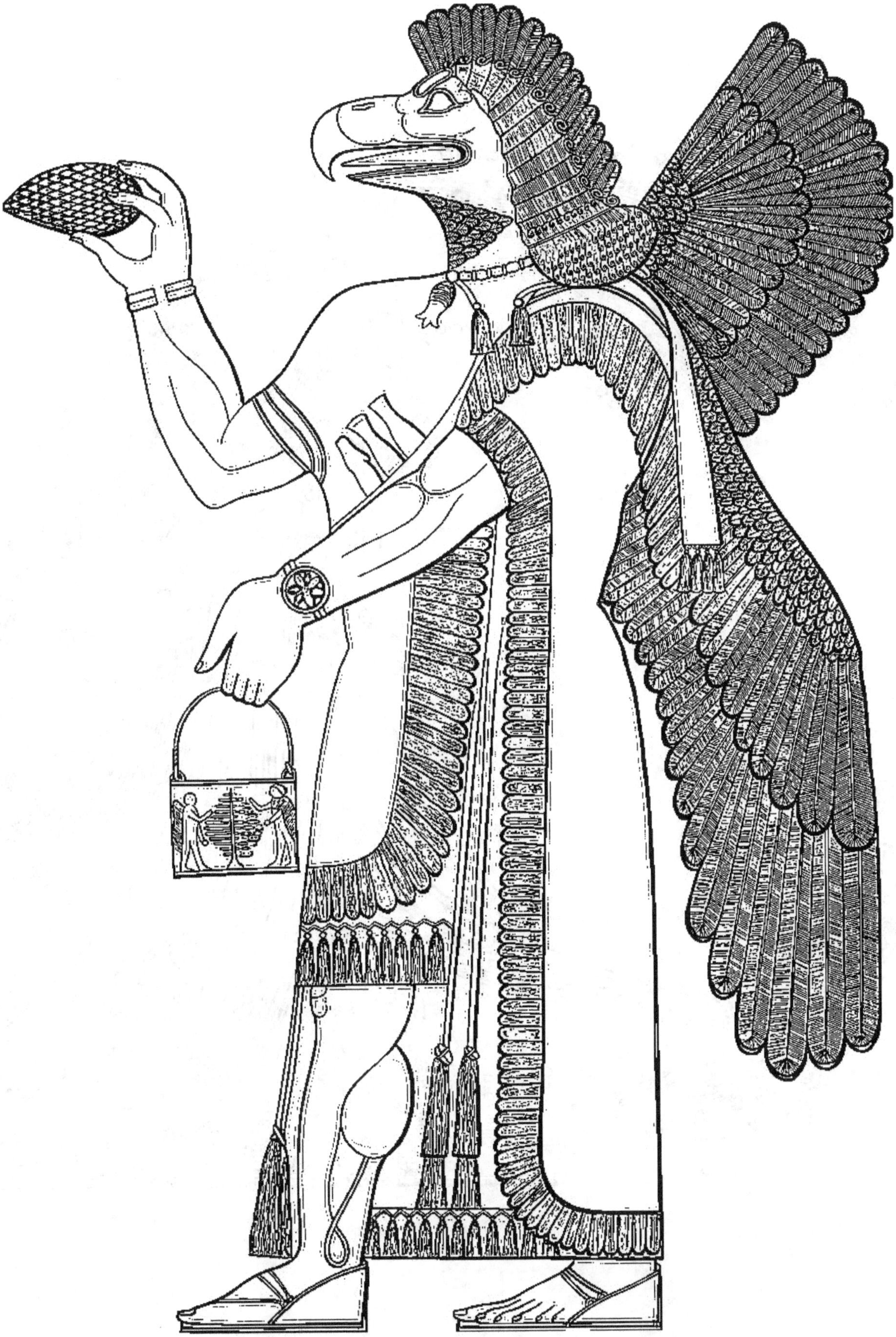

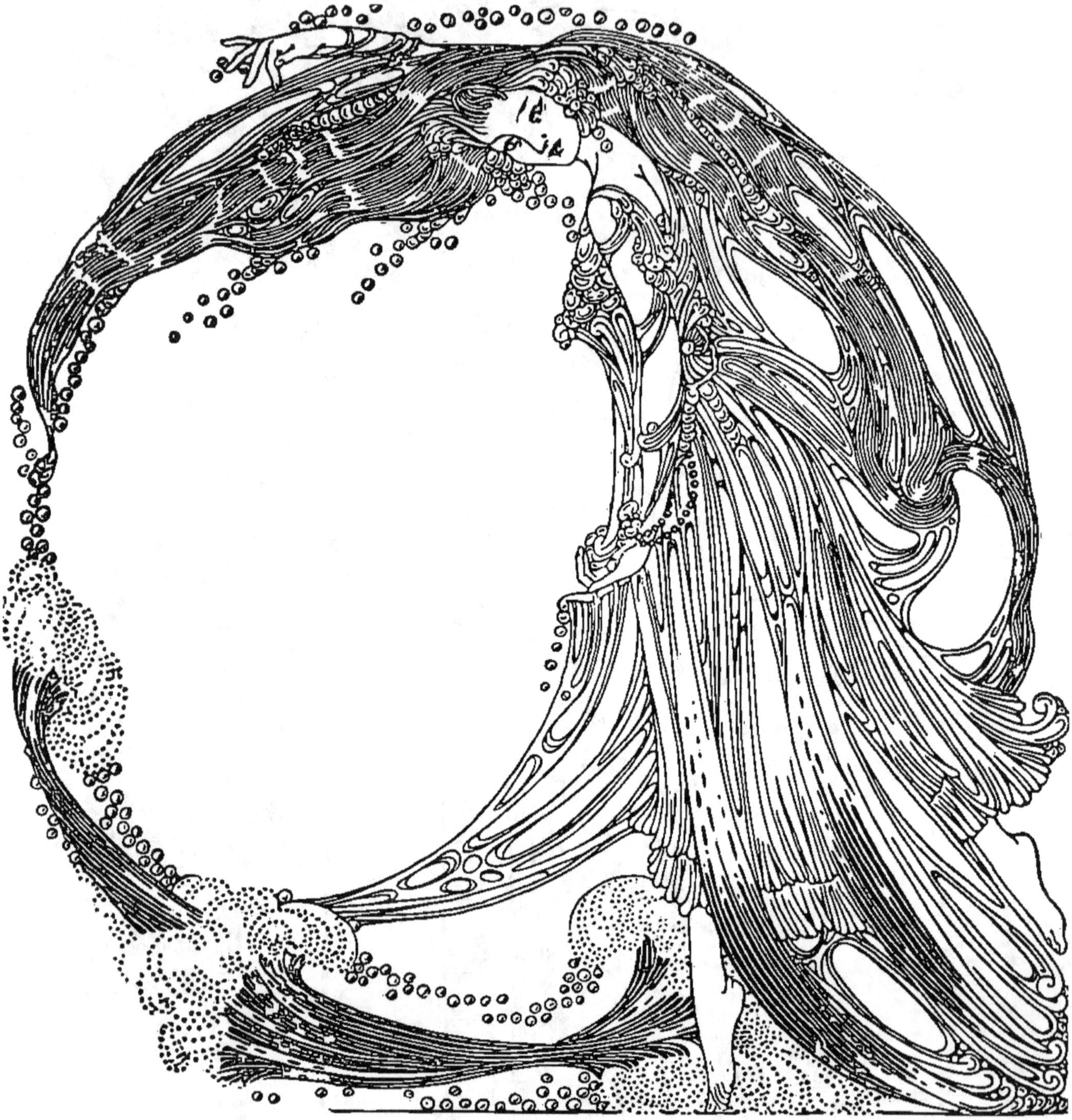

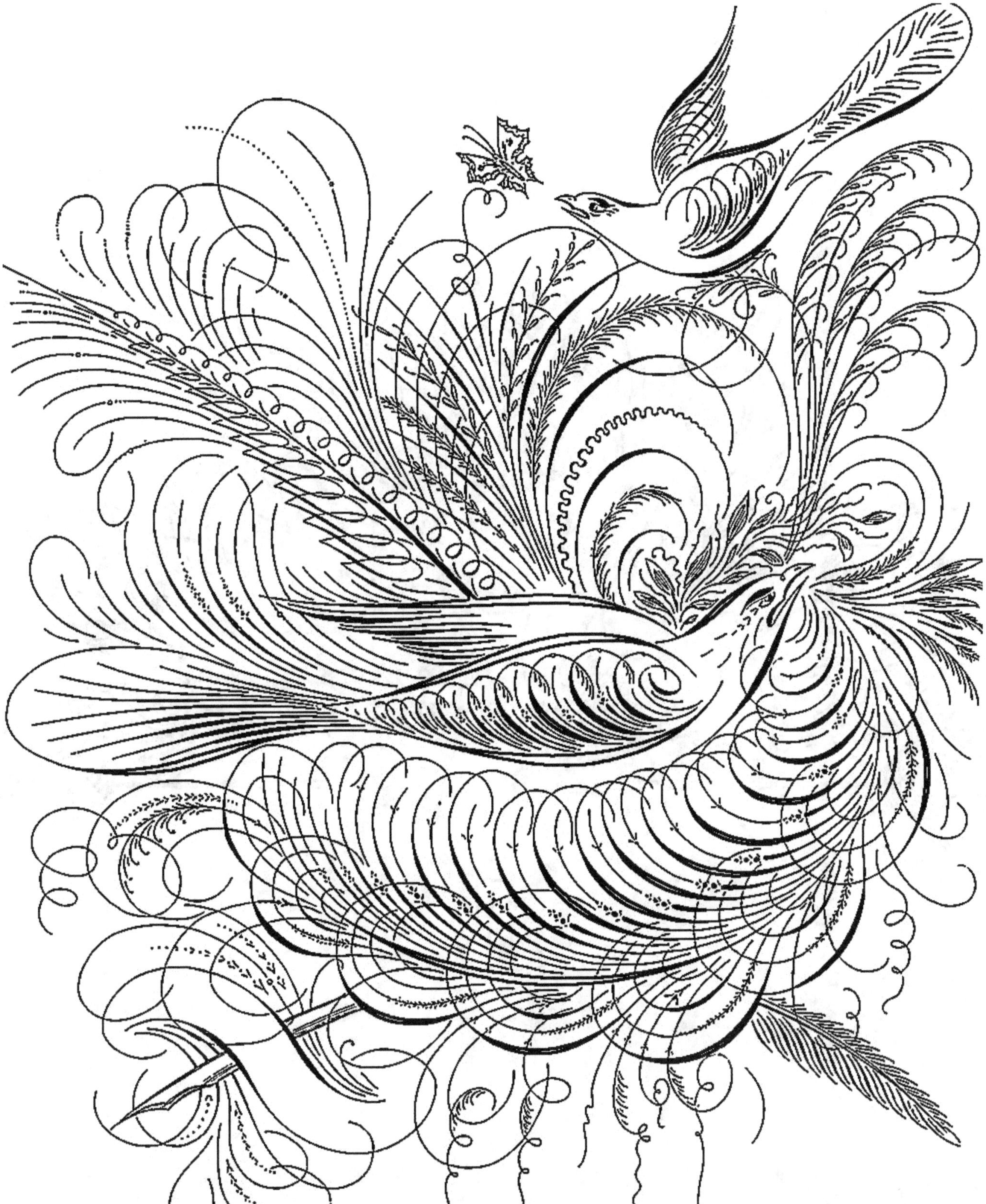

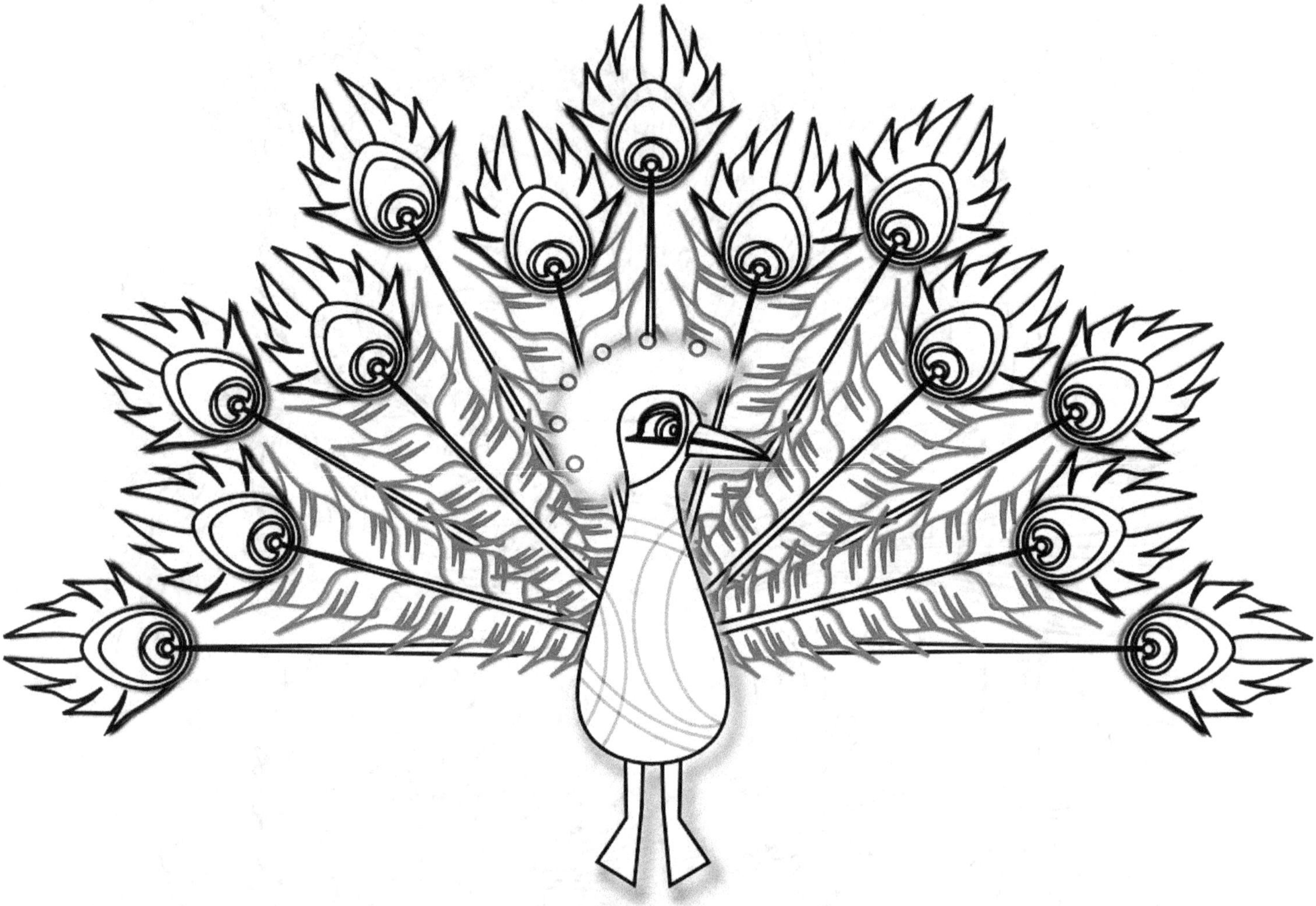

www.ingramcontent.com/pod-product-compliance
Lightning Source LLC
Chambersburg PA
CBHW060427220526
45465CB00008B/3046
* 9 7 9 8 6 4 0 3 1 4 3 7 3 *